*The frontispiece shows scenes from the needlelace
interpretation of Tennyson's poem* The Lady of
Shallot, *by Ros Hills (1987)*

# Needlelace Stitches

## CLASSIC AND CONTEMPORARY

Ros Hills
and
Pat Gibson

B. T. Batsford Ltd, London

# ACKNOWLEDGEMENT

It is with grateful thanks that we acknowledge help and encouragement from the following relatives, friends and professionals: Jim Gibson for photography, diagrams and tireless encouragement; Franta Provaznik for further photography; all those who kindly loaned their work for reproduction; and last, but not least, Jim's Macintosh computer for constantly and effortlessly reproducing the text.

The jacket shows
*front*
Point de Gaze style flower, leaf and bud taken from a piece of mid-nineteenth century lace. 12 cm × 11 cm, bud 3.5 cm × 2.5 cm (Pat Gibson, 1983); *Decorative rings* – stitches on a two-inch diameter ring (Ros Hills); Layered random loop stitches (Ros Hills, 1988); Close up: *A Summer in India* (Ros Hills, 1987)

*Back*
Blue Tit (life size) and pansy (Pat Gibson, 1983)

First published in 1989

ISBN 0 8521 9758 6

Typeset by Keyspools Ltd, Golborne
Printed in Hong Kong

for the Publishers
B. T. Batsford Ltd
4 Fitzhardinge Street
London W1H 0AH

A CIP record for this book is available from the British Library

# Contents

'And though our Country every where is fild
With Ladies, and with Gentlewomen, skild
In this rare Art, yet here they may diserne
Some things to teach them if they list to
    learne,
And as this booke some cunning workes doth
    teach
(Too hard for meane capacities to reach,)
So for weake learners, other workes here be,
As plaine and easie as are A B C.
Thus skilfull or unskilfull, each may take
This booke, and of it each good use may
    make.
All sorts of workes almost that can be nam'd
Here are directions how they may be fram'd:
And for this Kingdomes good are hither come
From the remotest parts of Christendome,
Collected with much paines and industry
From scorching *Spaine* and freezing *Muscovie*,
From fertill *France* and pleasant *Italy*,
From *Poland, Sweden, Denmarke, Germany*;
And some of these rare patternes have beene
    set
Beyond the bounds of faithlesse *Mahomet*:
From spacious *China*, and those Kingdomes
    East,
And from great *Mexico*, the Indies West.
Thus are these workes *farre fetcht and dearly
    bought*,
And consequently *good for Ladies thought*.
Nor doe I derogate (in any case)
Or doe esteeme of other teachings base,
For *Tent-worke, Rais'd worke, Laid-worke, Frost-
    worke, Net-worke*,
Most curious *Purles*, or rare *Italian Cut-worke*,
Fine *Ferne-stitch, Finny-stitch, New-stitch*, and
    *Chain-stitch*,
Brane *Bred-stitch, Fishes-stitch, Irish-stitch*, and
    *Queen-stitch*,
The *Spanish-stitch, Rosemary-stitch* and *Mowse-
    stitch*,
The smarting *Whip-stitch, Back-stitch*, and the
    *Crosse-stitch*;
All these are good, and these we must allow,
And these are every where in practise now:
And in this booke there are of these some
    store,
With many others neuer seen before.
Here Practise and Invention may be free;
And as a *Squirrell* skips from tree to tree,
So maids may (from their Mistresse, or their
    Mother)
Learne to leaue one worke, and to learne
    another,
For here they make choyce of which is which,
And skip from work to worke, from stitch to
    stitch,
Vntil, in time, delightfull practice shall
(With profit) make them perfect in them all.
Thus hoping that these workes may haue this
    guide,
To serue for ornament, and not for pride;
To cherish vertue, banish idlenesse,
For these ends, may this booke haue good
    successe.'

These words were written by John Taylor, the celebrated
Water-Poet, in his preface to the book called *The Needles
Excellency*, twelfth edition printed in 1640.

# Introduction

## Introduction

The delights of needlelace are many; not the least of these is discovering new stitch patterns to work. In this book you will find very familiar stitch patterns as well as ways of making more unusual patterns by taking a traditional method and using a contemporary thread or different spacing between stitches to create a 'new' effect. There are detailed stitch instructions and also line drawings to inspire you to work out your own ways of making a new stitch.

Step-by-step instructions are not always given, so that each person may put his or her individual knowledge and feeling for the work into operation. It is hoped that in this way new attempts will be made to try something out, working from the traditional into the unknown. It will also become apparent that there are no strict guidelines about choice of threads, so that you can experiment freely and venture into the exciting world of contemporary threads of all types.

To start with a single thread and finish with a decorative stitched textile is surely one of the joys of the work. Acquiring threads, in order to do this, in every shade, thickness, quality, texture and type has to be one of the greatest indulgences of anyone involved in the world of lacemaking – apart from buying books, that is! New threads produced by manufacturers are always examined and purchased with excitement. Old threads found in antique shops, jumble sales and even in granny's workbox are claimed like long-lost friends! Even though most lacemakers possess as much thread as they will ever need, they still cannot resist the opportunity to acquire more.

This book has been divided into separate chapters for different kinds of stitches. Each chapter contains both classical and contemporary interpretations of similar stitches. These have been deliberately combined in this way to aid the flow of your ideas and to give help when you get those 'what can I do next?' feelings! There are also line drawings of designs to make in needlelace. How these are best stitched is left to the reader to decide. No detailed advice has been given, so that every time a design is worked it will be different.

There are endless needlelace stitch patterns contained in many books, as well as a treasure trove to be found in old lace. This book brings together some of these stitch ideas to make a useful workbook that will also inspire yet more ideas that are uniquely of the late twentieth century.

# CHAPTER ONE

# *Loop stitches*

## The buttonhole stitch

This is one of the chief stitches to be found in all needlemade laces, known also as Close stitch or *Point Noné*. It is used for the raised part of designs known as the 'cordonnette', and also forms the basis for all the filling stitches used in this book.

**Fig 1** *Dove worked by Pat Gibson on the Advent altar cloth for the new chapel at St George's School, Ascot.*
*Featuring stripy filling, pea stitch variation 3a and overlapping picots on the eye couronne.*
*48 cm × 23 cm*

# Loop stitches

These stitches are all formed with one single loop or buttonhole stitch. The arrangement and grouping together of this stitch give various interesting effects. Some of the stitches are ideal for filling large areas, others are better suited to smaller spaces. Familiarity and practice will help in deciding which stitch to choose. It is very useful to prepare a sampler so that stitches may be tried prior to their use in the finished piece of work.

In order to reproduce the stitch as shown, it is essential to practise it first. Tension in this type of lace is very individual. A few simple guidelines can be given but each worker will find his or her own way of producing a stitch of satisfactory tension. When progressing from one stitch to the next do not leave too long a loop, because using this loop on subsequent rows will cause it to stretch and possibly pull other stitches out of shape. Do not, on the other hand, pull the stitches too tightly together. This will either cause a misshapen piece when the work is removed, or make it very difficult to find the correct loop for use in the next row of stitches. It is important to remember to whip down the cordonnet at the end of each row to allow for the height of the stitch.

## Point de Bruxelle (single Brussels stitch)

Work a foundation row of single loop stitches into the cordonnet. They should lie next to one another, not touching, but with barely space for a stitch between them.

**Row 1.** Whip down the cordonnet, bringing the needle out from underneath. Work one buttonhole stitch into each loop of the foundation row.

**Row 2.** Repeat row 1.

Continue in this manner backwards and forwards across the space to be filled, keeping the tension as even as possible.

If the area is uneven in shape, it will be necessary to increase or decrease the number of stitches on reaching the edge of the area.

**To increase:** Work extra stitches into the cordonnet, which are included in the next row. If this is not done an unsightly gap will appear between the last stitch and the cordonnet.

**To decrease:** Fasten into the cordonnet when reached, irrespective of the number of stitches in the previous row; continue as before.

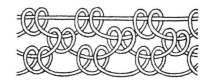

**Fig 3** *Double Brussels stitch*

## Double Brussels stitch

**Row 1.** Work two buttonhole stitches side by side into the cordonnet. Leave a space equal to the width of these two stitches, work another block of two. Repeat across the space. Fasten into the cordonnet. Whip down far enough to compensate for the depth of the stitch.

**Row 2.** Work two buttonhole stitches into the space between each block of two stitches on the previous row. Continue across the row. Repeat row 2 as often as is necessary to fill the space.

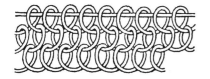

**Fig 2** *Single Brussels stitch*

**Fig 6** *Bee featured on the cushion in Fig 127.*

## Triple Brussels stitch (Greek Net Stitch)

This stitch is worked as for double Brussels stitch, but using blocks of three stitches.

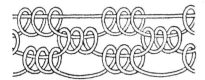

**Fig 4** *Treble Brussels stitch*

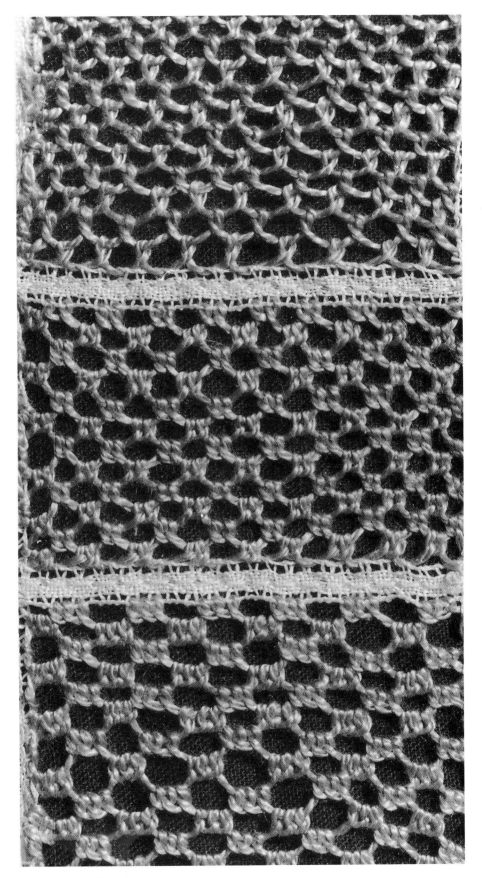

**Fig 5** *Single, double and treble Brussels stitch*

**Fig 7** Dragonbird, *a design to work as needlelace*

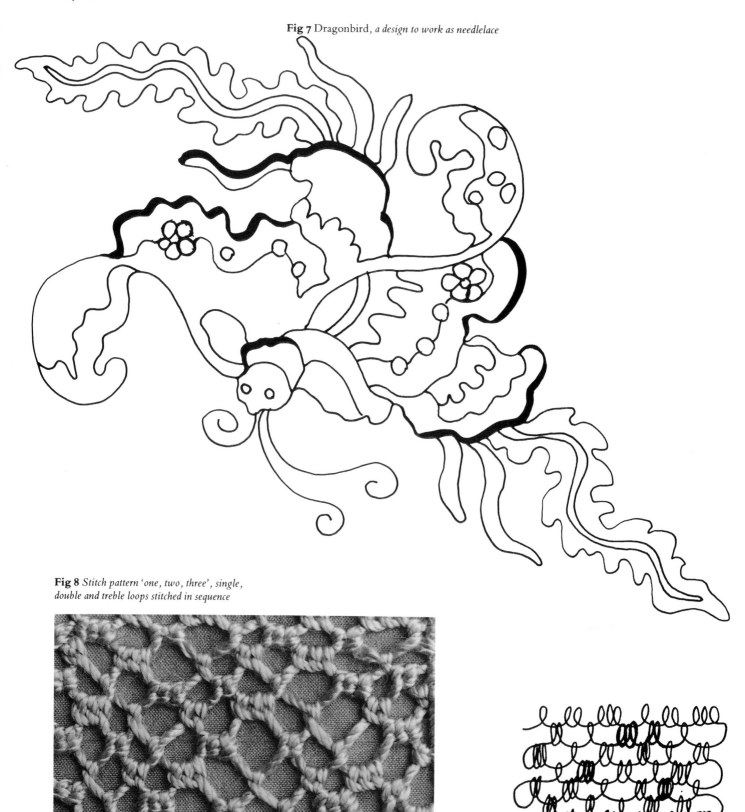

**Fig 8** *Stitch pattern 'one, two, three', single, double and treble loops stitched in sequence*

**Fig 9** *'One, two, three' stitch*

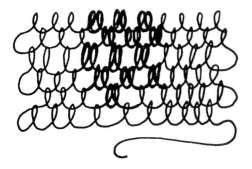

**Fig 10** *Double block: single loop stitch over an area with blocks of double loops at random*

**Fig 11** *Linen on perspex – abstract design in linen thread stretched over a sheet of perspex (Ros Hills)*

If you use a single loop stitch on its own or in groups of two or three, many varied patterns can be achieved. As well as making a single layer of stitches, several layers of stitchery could be put together, creating a dense textural effect.

# Pea stitches

## Basic stitch

**Row 1.** Work pairs of equally-spaced buttonhole stitches into the cordonnet.

**Row 2.** Work a single buttonhole stitch into the space between each group of pairs in the previous row.

**Row 3.** Work pairs of stitches into the loops formed in the previous row.

Continue to fill the space repeating rows 2 and 3 alternately.

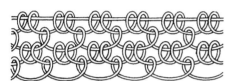

**Fig 12** *Pea stitch*

## Variation 1

This is the most popular of these stitches and is sometimes referred to as Point de Bruxelles.

**Row 1.** Work a row of equally-spaced buttonhole stitches across the top of the space to be filled.

**Row 2.** Work one stitch into each of the first two stitches of this row. ★ Miss two stiches, then work two. Repeat from ★ to the end of the row.

**Row 3.** Work one stitch in the loop between the pair of stitches, three stitches into the long loop; repeat to the end.

**Row 4.** Work one stitch into each loop formed by the group of three on the previous row (three stitches produce two loops), one long stitch across the pairs from row 2, repeat to end.

Repeat row 3.

The pattern is produced by repeating rows 3 and 4.

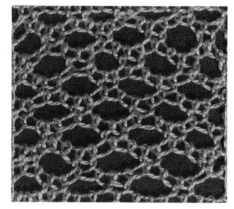

**Fig 13** *Pea stitch*

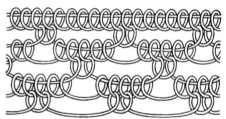

**Fig 15** *Pea stitch variation 1*

## Variation 2

**Row 1.** Work a row of close buttonhole stitches into the cordonnet.

**Row 2.** Work one stitch into each of the first two loops of the previous row. ★ Miss five loops. Work one stitch into each of the next two loops ★. Continue from ★ to the end of the row.

**Row 3.** Work five buttonhole stitches (giving four loops) into each long loop formed in Row 2.

**Row 4.** Work one stitch into each of the two adjacent centre loops of the block in the previous row. Continue in this manner to the end.

**Row 5.** Repeat row 3.

**Row 6.** Repeat row 4.

Continue repeating rows 3 and 4 until the space has been filled.

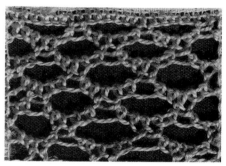

**Fig 16** *Pea stitch variation 2*

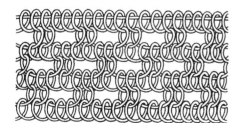

**Fig 17** *Pea stitch variation 2*

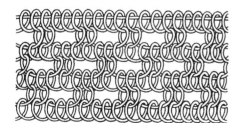

**Fig 14** *Pea stitch variation 1*

**Fig 18** *An unusual piece of tape lace found in the 'odds' box in an antique shop in Eton High Street. This piece has revealed several variations of some standard stitches, e.g. Eton stitch (Fig 84), Pea stitch variation 3a (Fig 23), pyramid stitch variation (Fig 48)*

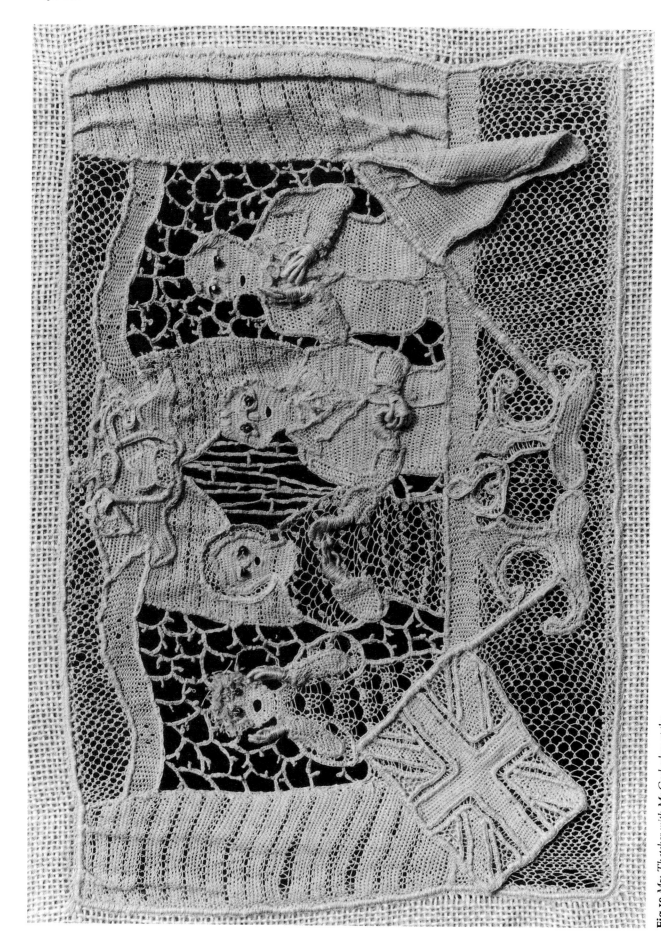

**Fig 19** *Mrs Thatcher with Mr Gorbachev at the Bolshoi (Ann Day, 1987). Needlelace panel, 14.5cm × 20cm*

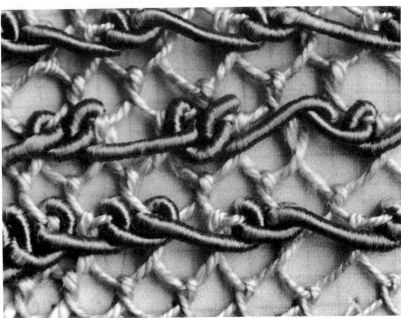

**Fig 20** *Layers of double loop stitch in various thicknesses*

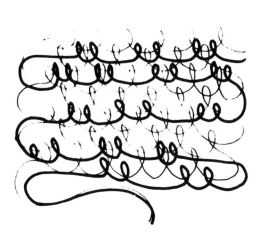

**Fig 21** *A ground of a single loop stitch. On top of this ground put in rows of double loop stitch*

**Fig 22** *Single loop stitch worked in linen with fine bullion cord worked as a second layer*

## Variation 3a

**Row 1.** Work a row of close buttonhole stitches into the cordonnet.

**Row 2.** Work one stitch into each of the first four loops of the previous row (three loops), miss three stitches, work four stitches.

Continue in this manner to the end of the row.

**Row 3.** Work five stitches (giving four loops) into the first long loop of the previous row. Work one stitch into the first loop of the group of four. Into the next stitch work a picot, then one further stitch into the third loop.

Continue across the row working a picot on the centre stitch of the groups of three loops.

**Row 4.** Work one stitch into each loop formed by the group of five of the previous row.

Continue across the row in this manner thus producing a long loop around the picot formed in the previous row.

**Row 5.** Repeat row 3.

**Row 6.** Repeat row 4.

Continue to fill the space by repeating rows 3 and 4.

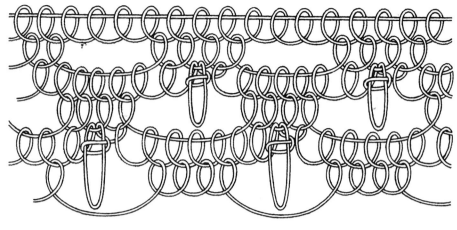

**Fig 23** *Pea stitch variation 3a*

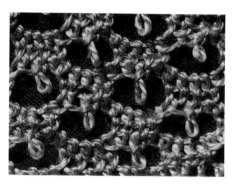

**Fig 24** *Pea stitch variation 3a*

## Variation 3b

**Row 3.** Instead of working a picot in the centre of the group of three, work a single Point de Venise stitch (Chapter 3 page 40).

Continue the rest of the sequence as for variation 3a, but using this substitution for row 3.

With a little experimenting other types of picot may well lend themselves for this area, e.g. a long Venetian picot (Chapter 7) or possibly even insert a bead at this point. When working with coloured threads, consider the possibility of changing colour for this row, or even changing the thickness of the thread.

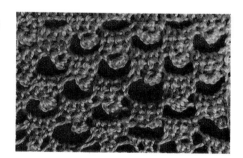

**Fig 25** *Pea stitch variation 3b*

## Variation 4

Work a foundation row as follows:
Into the cordonnet work ★ two
buttonhole stitches, leave a space
equivalent to two stitches, work two more
stitches, leave a space and work two more
stitches. Leave a space large enough to
accommodate six stitches ★ then continue
across the row from ★ to ★.

**Row 2.** Work two buttonhole stitches
into the gap between each group of two
on the previous row, six stitches into the
long loop, continue to the end of the row.

**Row 3.** ★ Work two stitches into the
space in the blocks of two stitches from
the previous row (only one space should
remain to be filled), two stitches into the
space before the block of six then one
stitch into each stitch of this block (five
stitches), two stitches into the next space.
Repeat from ★ to the end of the row.

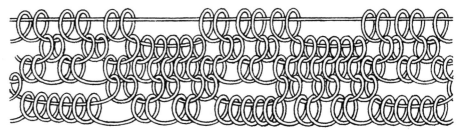

**Fig 26** *Pea stitch variation 4*

**Row 4.** ★ Work one stitch into each of
the first two loops of the block of nine
from the previous row, miss one, work
two, miss one, work two. Continue from
★ to the end of the row.

**Row 5.** Work as for row 2, the groups of
six stitches forming beneath the blocks of
twos of the previous rows.

Rows 2 to 4 inclusive form the pattern, so
these should be repeated as often as is
necessary in order to fill the available
space.

**Fig 27** *Pea stitch variation 4*

**Fig 28** *Butterfly showing: pyramid stitch,
pea stitch variation no. 1, Alençon beads, bar
cluster and long Venetian picots for the antennae
(Pat Gibson)*

**Fig 29** Russian Flowers, *a design to work as
needlelace*

**Fig 30** *Pea stitch with beads*

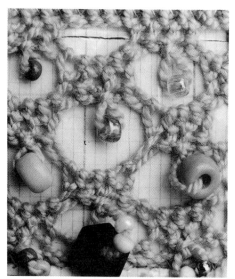

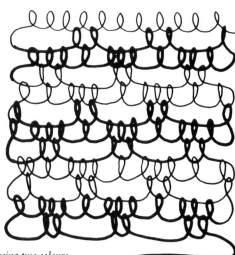

**Fig 31** *Pea stitch using two colours
of thread*

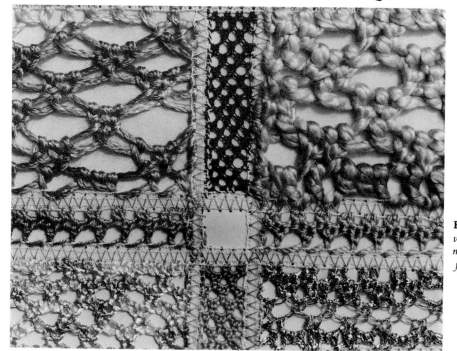

**Fig 32** *Sampler. Pea stitch in
various threads, thick silk,
metal, fine silk, man-made
fibre*

**Fig 33** Stitch on ground *(Ros Hills, 1987)*. *Loop stitches on and over fabric and wool strips*

## Point de Brabaçon

Commence from either right or left (left-handed people may wish to begin from left to right).

**Row 1.** Work one long and one short buttonhole stitch alternately to the end of the row. The long stitch should be sufficient to hold seven stitches.

**Row 2.** Work seven close buttonhole stitches into the long loop, one into the short loop. Continue in this manner to the end of the row.

**Row 3.** Work one buttonhole stitch on either side of the single stitch; this gives one long loop and one short loop as in row 1.

Repeat rows 2 and 3 until the space is filled.

The blocks of seven stitches should be arranged underneath each other in columns.

## Point de Brabaçon, variation 2a

Work from right to left.

**Row 1.** Work one long loop, two close buttonhole stitches, leave a small loop, then two close stitches, and another long loop. Repeat to the end.

**Row 2.** Work seven close stitches into the first long loop, two stitches into the small loop, seven into the next long loop. Continue to the end.

**Row 3.** Work two buttonhole stitches into each loop on either side of the group of two in the previous row.

Repeat rows 2 and 3.

## Variation 2b

Work the stitch as for variation 1 or 2a, but change row 2 as below:

**Row 2.** After two stitches into the long loop work a bullion knot (Chapter 8 page 140) or single picot (Chapter 8 page 137); work two more stitches, the chosen knot or picot and one more stitch (seven in all); two stitches into the space of two in the previous row. Continue in this manner to the end of the row.

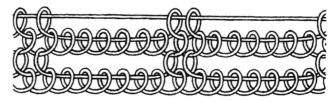

**Fig 34** *Point de Brabaçon*

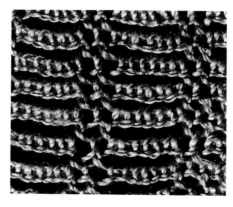

**Fig 35** *Point de Brabaçon*

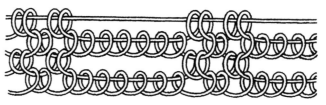

**Fig 36** *Point de Brabaçon variation 2a*

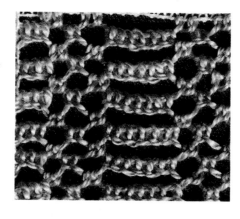

**Fig 37** *Point de Brabaçon variation 2a*

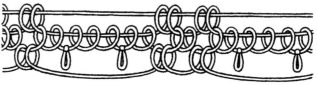

**Fig 38** *Point de Brabaçon variation 2b*

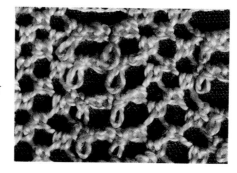

**Fig 39** *Point de Brabaçon variation 2b*

## Variation 3

This stitch appears as the ground stitch in a piece of early Belgian needlelace now in the possession of Exeter Museum. It needs to be worked in a fine thread between areas of much denser filled designs. It could be used as a filling stitch in its own right.

**Row 1.** Work two close buttonhole stitches, leave a space for two stitches then work another group of two stitches; leave a loop to take five stitches and continue with groups of two stitches across the row.

**Row 2.** ★ Work two stitches in the loop between groups of two; five stitches into the long loop ★. Continue from ★ to ★ to the end of the row.

**Row 3.** Work two stitches into the space before the block of five, one stitch into each loop of the block of five, two into the next loop (eight stitches). Continue across the row in this manner.

**Row 4.** ★ Miss the first loop of the block of eight stitches. Work one stitch into each of the next five stitches, miss one and

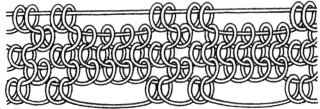

**Fig 40** *Point de Brabaçon variation 3*

**Fig 41** *Point de Brabaçon variation 3*

work two into the next loop. Continue from ★ to the end of the row.

**Row 5.** Work groups of two stitches on either side of the block of five as in row 1 (the foundation row).

Continue in this sequence, i.e. rows 2, 3, 4 and 5, until the area is filled.

**Fig 42** *A sampler based on a Honiton lace design, featuring pea stitch variation 1, point de Brabacon 2a and other stitches (Pat Gibson)*

**Fig 43** Stitch on Stitch 1 *(Ros Hills, 1987).*
*Layers of grid fabrics, felt, cotton, metallic,*
*detached buttonhole stitch added to make a focal*
*point. All fabrics dyed and spray dyed*

## Patterns for needlelace

These patterns have all been taken from pieces of seventeenth century gros point de Venise needlelace, held in the Victoria & Albert Museum in London.

## Suggestions for use

Take one motif and repeat it several times to make a border pattern, using different colours to make each motif. Choose several patterns to work together for edging table-linen. Increase the size of the motifs by using a photocopier, and make them up in very thick threads for decorating the front of a shopping-bag, beach bag or similar item. Make a mirror repeat and use to edge a plain roller blind. Take one motif, trace it off on to a piece of plain fabric, then move the fabric around to distort the shape. Trace this new shape off the fabric and stitch using metallic threads only. Mount this as a small picture or panel.

**Fig 44** *Stitch on Stitch 2 (Ros Hills, 1987)*
*Detached loop stitches in metal thread over grid*
*fabrics mounted on dyed calico*

**Fig 45** *Patterns for needlelace*

# Pyramid stitch (or butterfly stitch)

This is a useful stitch for filling a fairly large area.

Lay a foundation row of close, evenly-spaced buttonhole stitches.

**Row 1.** Miss ★ one stitch, work one stitch into each of the next five stitches, giving four loops, miss one, repeat from ★ to the end.

**Row 2.** Work one stitch into each of four loops of the previous row (three loops).

**Row 3.** As row 2, but with three stitches producing two loops.

Continue in this manner until only one stitch is worked forming the point of a triangle (two more rows)

**Row 6.** Work six buttonhole stitches into the long loops of the previous row.

Repeat from row 1 until the area is filled.

If the area to be filled is small, try making a smaller triangle by reducing the number of stitches in rows 1 to 5 or 4.

## Increasing and decreasing

It may be necessary to put an extra stitch into the cordonnet at the beginning or end of a row, where the area changes shape. If this is not done an unsightly and very large hole may result at the edge. The extra stitches will become part of the pattern as subsequent rows are worked.

## Pyramid stitch variation

Work the first group of the pyramids as for the basic stitch, i.e. a foundation row of either close, evenly-spaced buttonhole stitches or evenly-spaced loops, each loop to hold the required number of stitches for the widest part of the pyramid. Then work rows 1–5 inclusive.

**Row 6.** Work one triple point de Venise (see Chapter 3, page 40) into the long loop between each pyramid.

**NB:** Do not allow the loop from one stitch to the next to become too loose, as this will be pulled out of shape in subsequent rows.

**Row 7.** Work one single Brussels stitch (Fig 2) into each long loop of the previous row.

**Row 8.** Work six buttonhole stitches into each long loop of row 7.

Continue to fill the space following the instructions for the basic stitch, rows 2–5 inclusive.

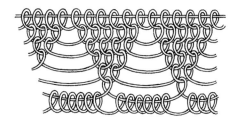

**Fig 46** *Pyramid stitch*

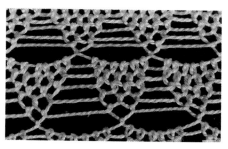

**Fig 47** *Pyramid stitch*

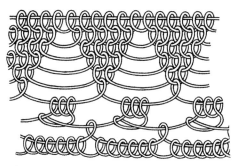

**Fig 48** *Pyramid stitch variation*

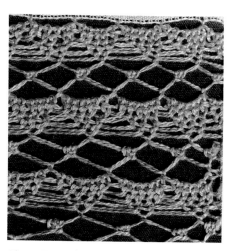

**Fig 49** *Pyramid stitch variation*

# Genoa stitch

Into the cordonnet:

**Row 1.** Work four buttonhole stitches, ★ leave a space equivalent to three stitches, work three stitches, leave a space of three, work four. Repeat from ★ until the space is filled.

**Row 2.** Make a group of nine stitches, three on either side of the group of four including the group of four. Miss three stitches (two loops) and repeat another group of nine stitches.

**Row 3.** Make nine stiches, three into the end of the group of nine, three into the long loop and three into the beginning of the next group of nine. Miss three stitches (two loops) and repeat.

**Row 4.** Repeat row 1, placing groups of three stitches in the long loops and groups of four stitches in the centre loops of the blocks of nine.

**Row 5.** As for row 2.

Continue to fill the space by working rows 2–4 inclusive.

The diamond effect made by the formation of the holes will only become apparent after completing row 5.

# Stripy filling stitch

**Row 1.** Work a row of close foundation stitches into the cordonnet.

**Row 2.** Work one stitch into each loop of the previous row.

**Row 3.** ★ Work one stitch into each of the adjacent loops of the previous row. Miss five loops, then repeat from ★ to the end of the row.

**Row 4.** Work two stitches into the centre of the long loop. Continue across the row in this manner.

**Row 5.** Work six stitches into each of the long loops and one stitch into the loop between the pairs of stitches from the previous row.

**Row 6.** As row 2.

Repeat rows 3 to 6 inclusive until the space has been filled.

**NB:** Do not make the long loop of row 3 too loose, as it will become looser on subsequent rows.

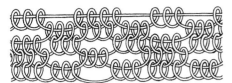

**Fig 50** *Genoa stitch*

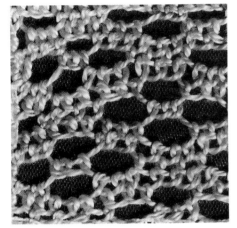

**Fig 51** *Genoa stitch*

## Point d'Anvers

This is a stitch frequently found in point lace, or tape lace, as it is now known.

**Row 1.** Work groups of three or four buttonhole stitches into the cordonnet leaving a space equivalent to that number of stitches between each group. Continue to the end of the row, working two or three stitches of the final group before taking the thread through the side cordonnet.

**Row 2.** Make one stitch into the first loop. Work one stitch into the long loop then one into each loop of the block of three or four, leave a loop and repeat to the end.

**Row 3.** Work one stitch into each loop of the block then one into the long loop, thus sloping the blocks of stitches to the right.

Continue in this manner, bringing in extra blocks of stitches on the left as space becomes available. The blocks may be sloped in the opposite direction by reversing the positioning of the stitch in the long loop.

This stitch may be further varied by whipping back through the loops, thus allowing the worker to form the stitches from whichever side he or she finds easiest. The instructions given above do not include the whipping.

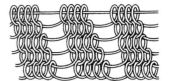

**Fig 55** *Point d'Anvers*

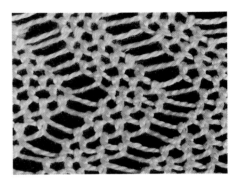

**Fig 56** *Point d'Anvers*

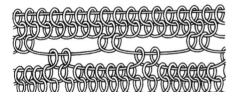

**Fig 53** *Stripy filling*

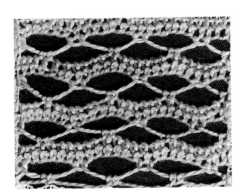

**Fig 54** *Stripy filling*

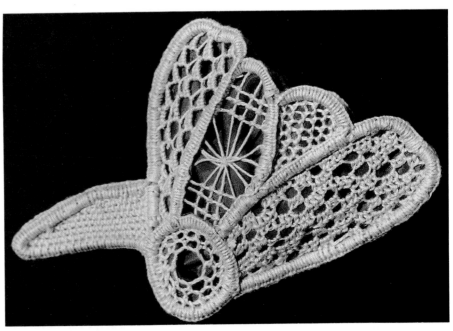

**Fig 52** *A purse using 12/2 linen thread showing Genoa stitch and a grid laid without any filling worked on to it*

27

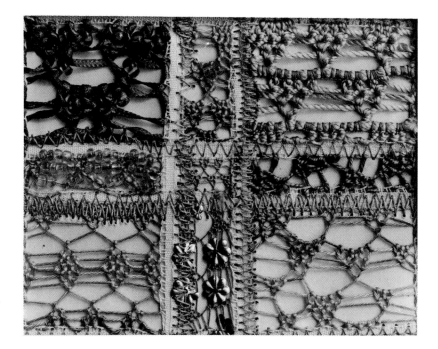

**Fig 57** *Sampler – pyramid stitch in ribbon, with beads and sequins*

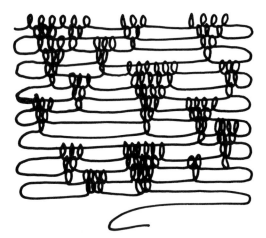

**Fig 58** *Random triangles*

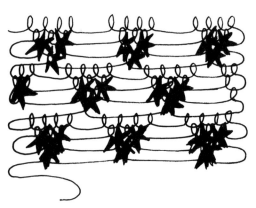

**Fig 60** *Triangles with sequins*

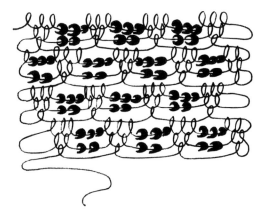

**Fig 59** *Triangles with beads on floats between*

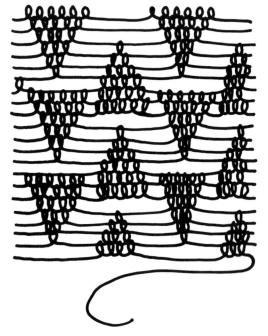

**Fig 61** *Up and down triangles*

**Fig 62** Essence of butterfly. *Make these designs in glowing butterfly colours, silk threads and the Madiera metallic embroidery threads. Mount the finished pieces in a metal grid to hang in a window*

## Point de Valencienne

Work a foundation row of close
buttonhole stitches.

**Row 1.** ★ Miss one, work two, miss one,
work five ★, repeat from ★ to ★ to the end
of the row.

**Row 2.** ★ Miss the first stitch of the block
of five, work two, miss one, two stitches
into the next loop of the previous row,
one into the group of two, then two into
the loop (forming a block of five). ★
Continue in this manner to the end of the
row.

**Row 3.** Work two stitches into the loop
before the block of five, one stitch into
each loop and two into the next loop
(block of eight). Continue across the row
working blocks of eight stitches.

The diamonds either increase or decrease
as shown by the following sequence of
numbers:

```
      5   2   5
    2   5   2
          8
    2   5   2
      5   2   5
      8       8
```

After each block there should be a space
achieved by missing one stitch in the row
above. The spaces form diamond patterns
throughout the area.

**NB:** The traditional Gros Point
Diamond, the stitch found in profusion in
early Venetian Gros Point lace, is formed
with a 3, 8, 13, 8, 3 stitch sequence using a
point d'Espagne stitch, and often
incorporating a cord.

Point de Valencienne achieves the same
effect but is simpler to follow. It is also
possible to work a corded version of this
stitch, as seen in the sample illustrated in
Chapter 3.

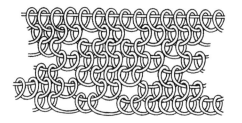

**Fig 63** *Point de Valencienne*

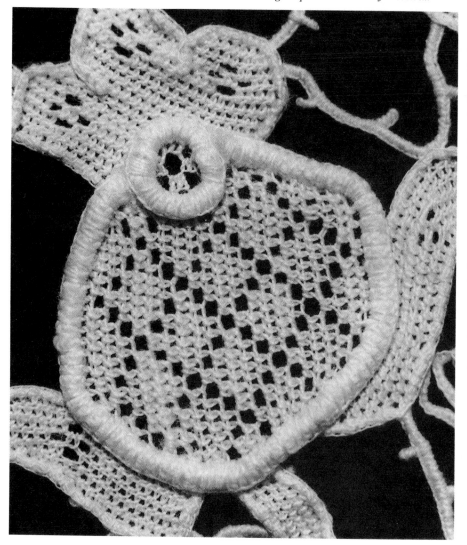

**Fig 64** *Point de Valencienne shown here worked in
a motif from a piece of Burano needlepoint lace,
imitating early Venetian lace. 1.5 cm × 1.6 cm*

# Burano stitch

Lay a foundation row of equally-spaced buttonhole stitches along the chosen edge. It is sometimes easier to begin with the longest straight edge in the area to be filled. This is, of course, dependent upon the stitch and the effect required.

**Row 1.** Work two buttonhole stitches into each of the first two loops. Miss three loops and repeat to the end.

**Row 2.** Work five buttonhole stitches into each long loop of row 1.

**Row 3.** Work one buttonhole stitch into each loop of the group of five on row 2 (four loops).

**Row 4.** Work four buttonhole stitches over the long loops of the previous row.

**Row 5.** Repeat row 2.

**Row 6.** Repeat row 3.

Rows 4, 5 and 6 form the pattern and should be repeated as often as is required to fill the space.

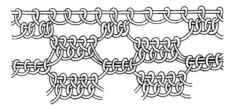

**Fig 65** *Burano stitch*

**Fig 66** *Burano stitch*

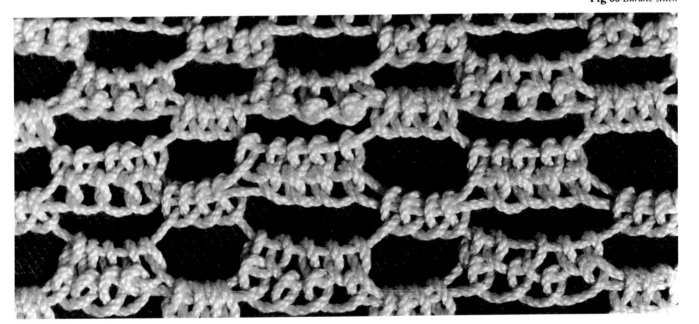

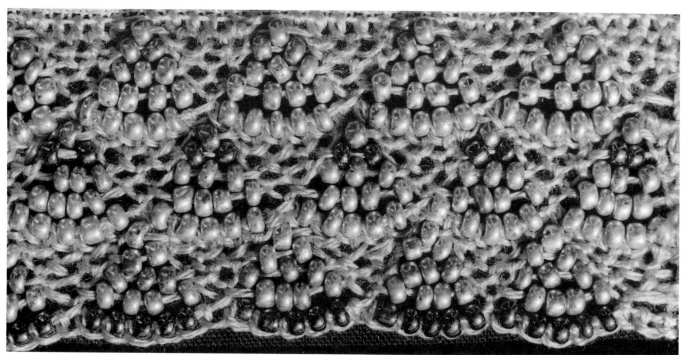

**Fig 67** *A Burano copy of a piece of Flemish
needlelace, 8.5 cm wide.*

**Fig 68** *Pyramid stitch variation with beads*

**Fig 69** Audition, *3D needlelace in the style of seventeenth-century English needlelace (Susan Oneal, 1988). Approx 9 cm high*

33

# CHAPTER TWO

# Twisted stitches

## Point d'Espagne (English stitch, or hollie stitch)

There are several different names for this stitch, depending upon the type of lace in which it is found. There are also a number of different ways of forming the stitch, but the resulting twisted effect is the same. It is up to the worker to experiment to find the system that works most satisfactorily for him or her.

(**NB:** There is no explanation given for working the stitch in the Continental manner.)

**Method 1.** (From left to right.) Pass the needle over and under the cordonnet. Wrap the thread from the eye of the needle left to right under the point of the needle. Pass the point of the needle under the thread from the previous stitch. Pull up (Fig 70).

(If working from right to left, pass the thread from the eye of the needle from right to left.)

**Method 2.** Work a single buttonhole stitch, going over and under the cordonnet (see Fig 72). Pass the needle from right to left through the resulting loop and ease up. Reverse from right to left.

**Method 3.** Place the left thumb over the working thread, then wrap the thread around the thumb from right to left. Take the needle through the loop and thread crossing the thumb. Pull up (Fig 73). Wrap the thread around the thumb regardless of which direction the stitch is being worked.

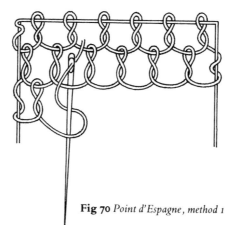

**Fig 70** *Point d'Espagne, method 1*

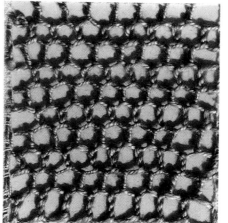

**Fig 71** *Point d'Espagne, method 1*

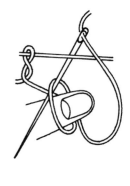

**Fig 73** *Point d'Espagne, method 3*

## Whipped stitch variations

Work a row of point d'Espagne stitches, then whip into the loops between the stitches. Work the next row of stitches incorporating the whipping and loop of the previous row. This gives a firm edge if working around an area to be filled with a closer stitch, e.g. single corded Brussels stitch. It may also be used to decorate the inside edge of a flower petal while leaving the rest of the space open. The worker forms the stitch in the same direction each time.

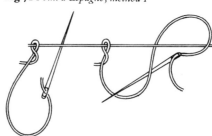

**Fig 72** *Variations of working point d'Espagne, method 2*

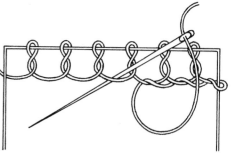

**Fig 74** *Point d'Espagne, whipped stitch variation*

## Point de Greque

**Row 1.** Work three point d'Espagne stitches close together. Leave a space equivalent to three stitches. Work another group of three. Continue in this way across the row.

**Row 2.** Work three stitches into the loops between the stitch blocks of the previous row.

Repeat these two rows until the area is filled.

At the end of row 1 a cord may be laid back across the area, then row 2 is worked picking up the loop and cord of the previous row.

As this thread is laid across it may be whipped into the stitches of the previous row if wished.

## Combination loop and whipped stitch

Work two rows of single corded Brussels stitch (see Chapter 4).

**Row 3.** Work one point d'Espagne stitch into alternate loops of the previous row.

**Row 4.** Work two stitches into each loop of the previous row, lay back a cord. Continue to work repetitions from row 2 until the area is filled.

Variations of this stitch can be adopted by working more rows of single corded Brussels stitch between the open rows. Work as above, but whip the laid cord through the loops of the stitches to be missed.

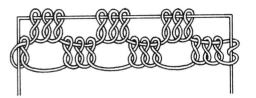

**Fig 75** *Point de Greque*

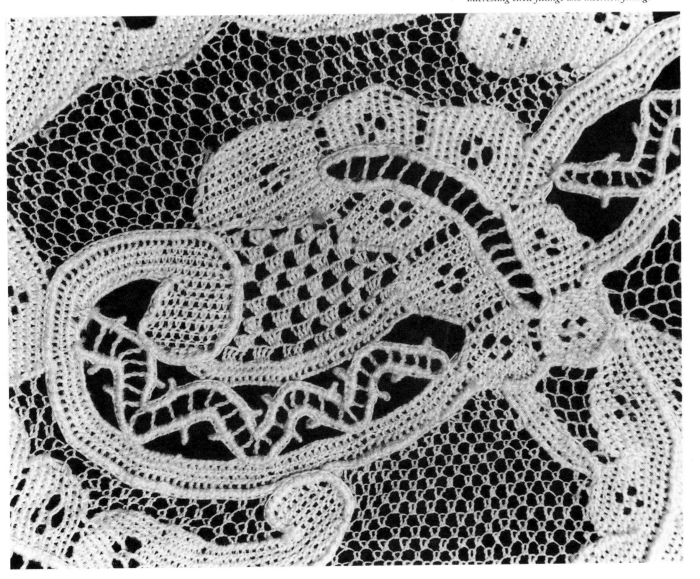

**Fig 76** *Point de Greque: also showing some interesting circle fillings and insertion fillings*

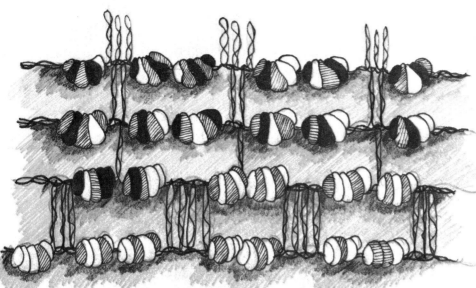

**Fig 77** *Twist and bell. Twisted stitches with groups of buttonhole stitches on bars between single stitches*

**Fig 78** *1. Make a row of twisted stitches in a row of three or four stitches*
*2. Whip back over and under the long loops*
*3. Make groups of buttonhole stitches on the long bars in between the twisted stitches in the manner of cinq point groups*

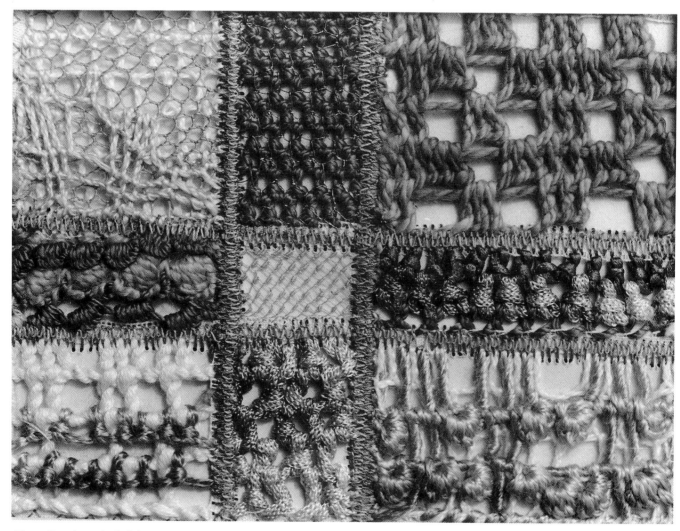

**Fig 79** *Sampler: twisted stitches*

**Fig 80** Chinese flowers, *flower design taken from an antique Chinese embroidery, to work as needlelace*

**Fig 81** Needle and bobbin lace mix *(Pauline Sutton, 1987). 12 cm × 12 cm*

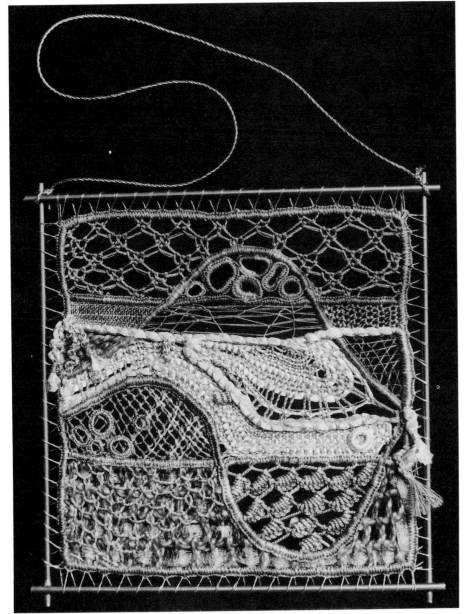

**Fig 82** *Combination single corded Brussels and point d'Espagne. Ideal for producing a row of holes in the design or a leaf vein*

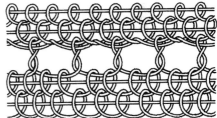

**Fig 83** *As Fig 82, but the laid cord is whipped before working point d'Espagne*

## Eton stitch

**Row 1.** Work seven close buttonhole stitches, then leave a space for six stitches. Repeat to the end of the row.

**Row 2.** Work one stitch into each loop of the block of seven (six stitches), then whip four or five times along the loop. Repeat into the next block of seven, continue to the end of the row.

**Row 3.** Work seven stitches into the block, i.e. one stitch into the end of the long loop, five into each stitch of the block and one into the beginning of the next long loop. Work one point d'Espagne stitch into the centre of the long loop. Continue in this manner to the end of the row.

**Row 4.** Work three stitches on either side of the point d'Espagne of the previous row, and one into each loop of the block. Continue to the end of the row.

**Row 5.** Work blocks of seven stitches as in row 1, but underneath the holes of the previous pattern.

Repeat from row 2 (See Fig 18).

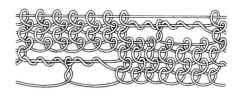

**Fig 84** *Eton stitch*

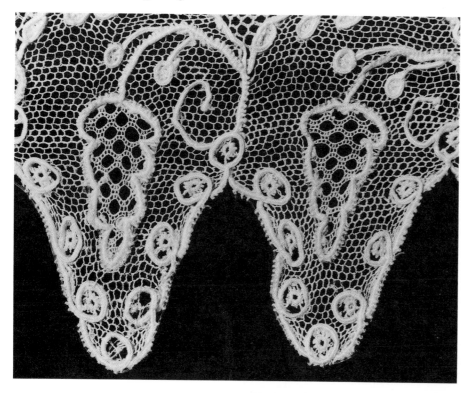

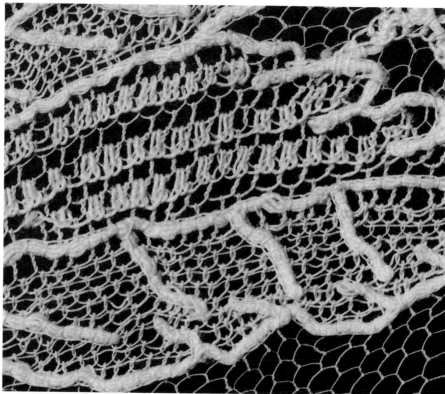

**Fig 86** *From a piece of nineteenth-century point de gaze, showing rows of double Brussels stitch worked over point d'Espagne to give shaded effect*

**Fig 85** *A piece of early Alençon needlepoint lace, featuring pea stitch formation using a twisted stitch. Horsehair is apparent in the picots. Each scallop is 2.5 cm × 4.5 cm*

**Fig 87** *Mid nineteenth-century point de gaze,
featuring point d'Angleterre wheels and Ardenza
bar (the latter worked over the mesh ground of point
d'Espagne). Note a variation of stripy filling: six
rows of single corded Brussels stitch, five rows of
point d'Espagne; the centre row is overstitched
using single Brussels, three into each loop*

**Fig 88** *A much enlarged point de gaze flower,
design taken from an old piece of lace, worked in
linen thread 12/2. The cordonnet was laid using a
fine twisted twine and two further strands were laid
before buttonholing the cordonnette. Attached to a
handbag of closely woven hessian (Pat Gibson,
1984)*

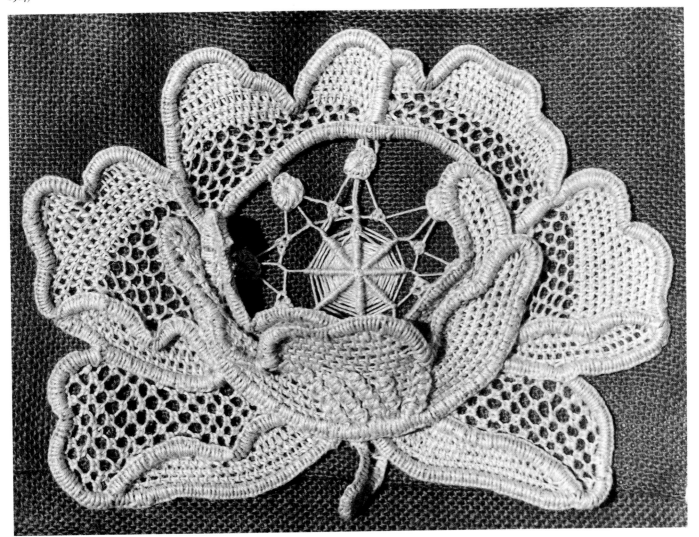

# CHAPTER THREE

# Knotted stitches

## Knot stitch

The stitch is required when laying threads straight across the area to be filled, e.g. in square mesh fillings to create a net, and in wheel fillings for laying in the rays. It may also be used when fastening threads at the beginning and end of rows of stitches.

Lay the thread straight across to the point of knotting. Insert the needle to the outside of the thread and under the cordonnet.
Loop the thread under the point of the needle.
Pull up tightly. If the needle is slipped into the loop of the knot as it is being tightened and held away from the cordonnet, the resulting cord will lie taut across the space.

## Point de Venise

There are numerous variations of this stitch. Used singly it could form a mesh background; alternatively, double or triple stitches make attractive fillings.

## Single point de Venise

Attach the working thread to the top left of the cordonnet, make a buttonhole stitch and pull up fairly tightly. Lay the thread from this stitch to the left, hold firmly in place with the left thumb (right thumb if left-handed), place the needle behind the loop of the previous stitch and under this thread, and pull up tightly to form a knot. Continue across the space to be filled. Working from right to left,

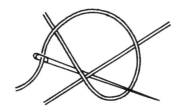

**Fig 89** *Knot stitch*

**Fig 90** *Sampler showing the Brussels stitches and the point de Venise variations (Pat Gibson)*

work the stitch and lay the thread to the right in order to form a knot.

## Double point de Venise

Work groups of two buttonhole stitches into the cordonnet close together. Then work the knot as given for single point de Venise.

This stitch forms a rectangular block which can be lengthened by working two knot stitches into the loop. Further

**Fig 91a** *Single point de Venise, stitch formation*

**Fig 91b** *Single point de Venise, the completed stitch*

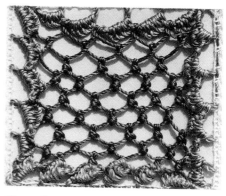

**Fig 92** *Cinq point de Venise filled with single point de Venise*

permutations of this stitch are possible, but it is advisable to try samples first to determine the effect they will give.

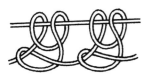

**Fig 93** *Double point de Venise*

**Fig 94** *Double point de Venise, variation*

**Fig 97** *Cinq point de Venise*

**Fig 95** *Double point de Venise, variation*

## Cinq point de Venise

Work a row of spaced foundation stitches into the cordonnet from *right to left*.

**Row 2.** ★ Work one stitch into the first loop, take the thread back along this stitch, make a knot stitch as shown in Fig 89, then three or four more stitches over both threads, working back towards the original stitch. This forms a small scallop. If the first and last stitches are pulled a little tighter than the rest, the scallop shape will be more pronounced and pleasing. Try using a different colour or texture for this row.

**Row 3.** Work a stitch into the space between each cluster of stitches on the previous row.

Repeat from ★.

## Cinq point de Venise: variation

Instead of working row 3, repeat row 2 in the opposite direction.

The variation in Fig 92 may be used to fill an area with differing textures. The outer border all around is worked with cinq point de Venise. The centre is filled with any of the following stitches: single Brussels, point de Feston, single point de Venise.

**Fig 98** *Cinq point de Venise*

**Fig 96** *Double point de Venise, variation*

**Fig 99** *Cinq point de Venise made using metallic ribbon and thick silk*

**Fig 100** *Patterns – beating wings. Stitch in neutral colours in one stitch using different thicknesses of thread. Use only cinq point de Venise but vary the size and spacing of the stitches*

**Fig 101a** *Stitch patterns. a) Layers of loop stitches using the belle from the belle point de Venise stitch as a surface texture*

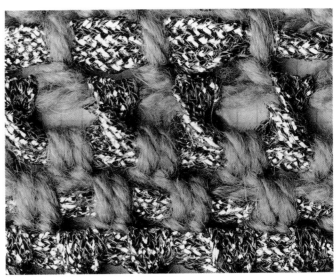

**Fig 101b** *Point de Turque in metal ribbon and heavy silk thread*

**Fig 101c** *Point de Turque*

**Fig 101d** *Petit point de Venise made in tape, bullion cord and silk*

## Belle Point de Venise

This is another variation of the cinq point de Venise range of stitches.

Work a foundation row of spaced buttonhole stitches, each loop long enough to take four stitches.

**Row 1.** Work four buttonhole stitches into each loop along the row.

**Row 2.** Work one stitch into the loop between each stitch of the previous row (three stitches).

**Row 3.** Work one stitch into each loop of the resulting pyramid (two stitches). Before moving on, take the thread back to the loop from the previous group of stitches and work four or five loop stitches on this thread. Pull the last stitch firmly and the group should form a semi-circle. Continue on to the next group of stitches and repeat.

**Row 4.** Lift each shell and work a stitch into the loop between the two stitches of the previous row.

Repeat the stitch sequence, rows 1–4 inclusive.

**Variation:** The sample has been worked using thread of different thicknesses. It will be necessary to fasten off and rejoin yarn to the correct side as the work progresses.

If you wish the shells to lay flat then row 4 should be worked by placing the stitches in the loops between each shell instead of beneath them.

Many interesting variations are possible using metallic threads for the base stitches and working beads into the shell.

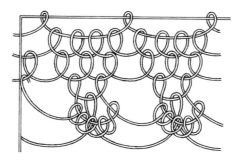

**Fig 102** *Belle point de Venise*

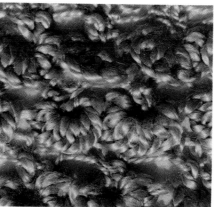

**Fig 103** *Belle point de Venise*

## Point de Feston

This stitch is similar in appearance to single point de Venise.

**Row 1.** Work a single Brussels stitch into the cordonnet and take the needle back behind the stitch just formed and in front of the thread, thus forming a knot. Continue across the row in this manner, spacing the stitches evenly.

**Row 2.** Return, forming the stitch in the same way as in row 1, but placing each stitch in the loops between the stitches.

**NB:** Do not leave any slack between one stitch and the next. This will make the stitches sag and look uneven.

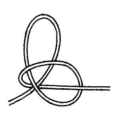

**Fig 104a** *Point de Feston*

**Fig 104b** *Point de Feston*

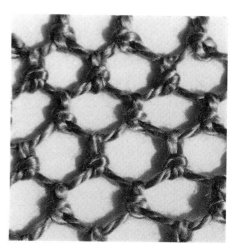

**Fig 105** *Point de Feston*

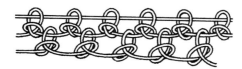

**Fig 104** *Point de Feston*

**Fig 106** *A flower, leaves and stems from a mid nineteenth century piece of point de gaze needlelace, featuring Ardenza bar, four-hole bud, point d'Angleterre and point d'Espagne ground*

**Fig 107** *A mat design taken from an old piece of
needlelace, but with a new choice of filling stitches
(Sissy Maynard, 1987). 25 cm × 25 cm*

**Fig 108** *Needlelace panel (Jane Meade, 1987)*

## Ardenza point

Fasten the working thread into the left-hand vertical cordonnet.

**Row 1.** ★ Work a single loop stitch into the horizontal or top cordonnet. Pass the thread in a loop up and over the top. Place the needle into the cordonnet from underneath, pull upwards with the thread behind the needle, then pull downwards to lock the stitch in place.

The next stitch is worked so that it leaves a space equivalent to the width of the previous stitch. Continue from ★ to the end of the space.

**Row 2.** Work the same stitch into the loop between stitches on the previous row.

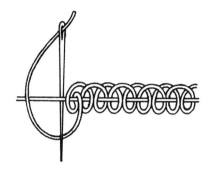

**Fig 109** *Ardenza stitch*

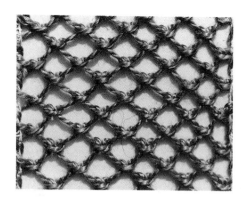

**Fig 111** *Ardenza point*

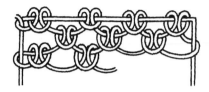

**Fig 110** *Ardenza point*

**Fig 112** *Ardenza bar*

## Ardenza bar

This is Ardenza point stitch worked so that the loops appear on both sides of the cordonnet. It is a very useful stitch for creating veins on leaves and petals and for stems. It may be worked directly over the cordonnet or over extra laid threads. The stitch is often found worked directly on to net, particularly in Point de Gaze lace, where the net ground fills the spaces between flowers. Tiny buds and stems are then worked directly on to the net filling.

The stitch is formed in exactly the same way as Ardenza point stitch. Proceed along one side of the stem or vein, then return along the other side, placing stitches in the spaces between stitches from the opposite edge. Be careful not to catch in the loop on the opposite edge.

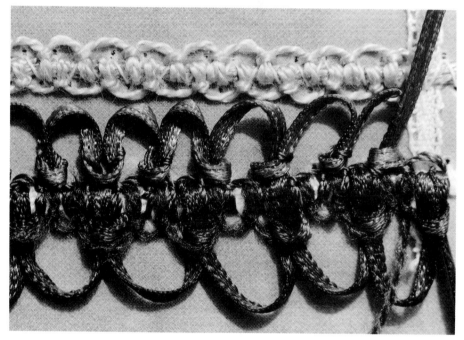

**Fig 113** *Ardenza bar using different threads (Pat Gibson)*

*Stitches made with textured knitting yarns*
*(Ros Hills)*

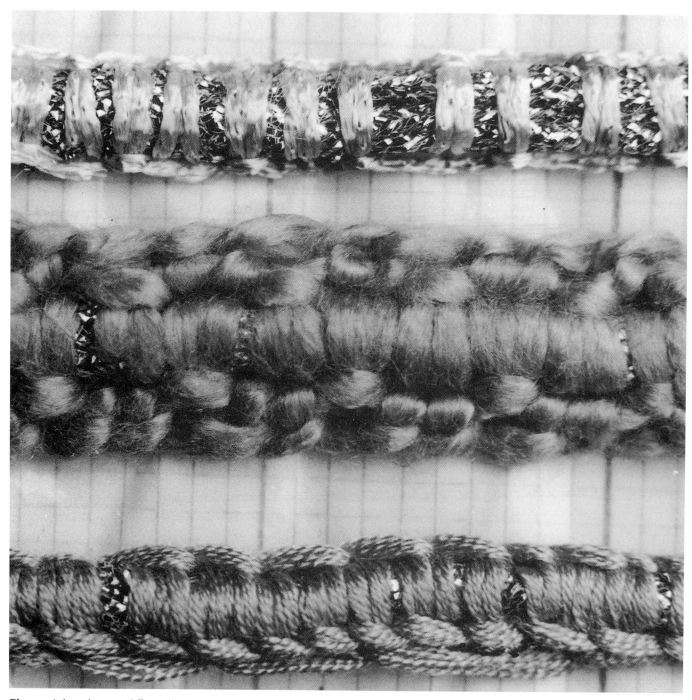

**Fig 114** *Ardenza bar using different threads*
*(Ros Hills)*

## Point de Sorrento

There are many variations of this stitch. Most of them are different combinations of a loop stitch, but the one described here has a knot which holds the stitch in position. At a quick glance it could be mistaken for a single or double Brussels stitch.

**Row 1.** Work a single loop stitch into the cordonnet, then knot it by passing the needle a second time through the same loop. Draw it up tightly before commencing the next stitch.

**Row 2.** The same stitch is worked into the spaces between the stitches of the previous row.

**Variation:** If the initial loop of the stitch is made longer then it is possible to work between the two threads of the buttonhole stitch of the previous row. The stitches lie in vertical lines instead of an alternating pattern. See Fig 118.

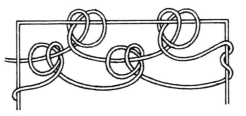

**Fig 115** *Point de Sorrento*

**Fig 117** *Point de Sorrento*

**Fig 116** *Point de Sorrento, forming the stitch*

**Fig 118** *Point de Sorrento*

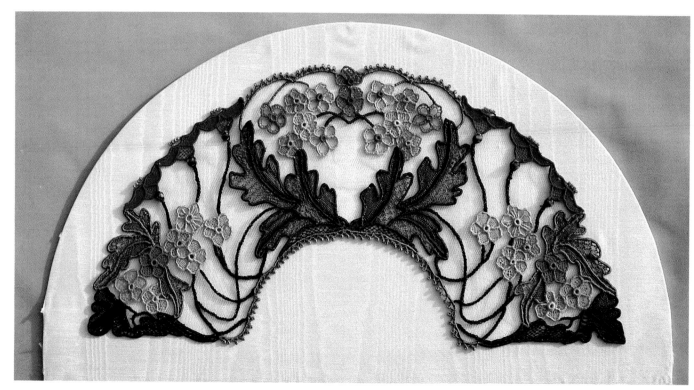

A fan leaf, based on the design by Louisa and
Rosa Tebbs in one of their bobbin lace books.
(Pat Gibson, completed 1987)

*A Summer in India, needlelace collage (Ros Hills) 50cm × 40cm*

# CHAPTER FOUR

# Corded stitches

## Single corded Brussels stitch

This stitch is the one that appears as the solid areas on very early needlepoint lace.

Those who find it difficult to work the stitches from both left and right should find this one a little easier, as it is worked in one direction only. The choice of direction depends upon whether the worker is right- or left-handed.

**Row 1.** Work a foundation row of close buttonhole stitches into the cordonnet. Whip the thread under and over the cordonnet, then lay it back across the space. Fasten under and over the cordonnet. This thread should lie just below the loops of the previous row.

**Row 2.** Work a buttonhole stitch through the first loop of the previous row and under the laid thread. Continue across the row, working one stitch into each one of the previous row. Miss the last loop of the previous row unless the space is increasing in size. Whip the thread under the cordonnet and lay it back across the space, fastening into the cordonnet on the other side of the space.

**Row 3.** Repeat row 2 until the space has been filled.

## Double corded Brussels stitch

Work as for the single corded stitch, but use blocks of two stitches, leaving sufficient space between them to accommodate a block of two.

Lay the thread back and work blocks of two stitches into the spaces and into the cord.

**NB:** From row 3 onwards *do not* pick up the cord from the previous row where it lies under a block of stitches. If this is done the appearance of the stitch will be totally different, which may be desirable in some instances.

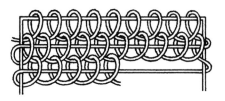

**Fig 119** *Single corded Brussels stitch*

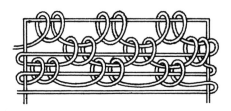

**Fig 120** *Double corded Brussels stitch*

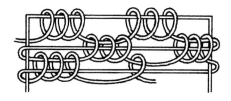

**Fig 121** *Treble corded Brussels stitch*

## Treble corded Brussels

This is worked as for the previous stitches in this section but using blocks of three stitches.

**Variation:** Alternate the rows of treble corded Brussels stitch with a row of single corded Brussels stitch (see Fig 122).

## Four-hole bud

This feature can be used anywhere to break up an area of solid corded stitching.

**Row 1.** Decide upon the position of the first hole, work along the row, miss one loop and continue to the end of the row.

**Row 2.** Lay the thread across, work corded stitch until reaching one stitch before the hole of the previous row. Miss this stitch, work two stitches into the loop including the cord, miss one and continue to the end of the row.

**Row 3.** Lay the thread across, work as far as the first hole, two stitches into the loop, miss the next loop, two stitches into the loop, and continue to the end.

**Row 4.** Lay the thread across and work a complete row of stitches (remember to work two stitches into the loop).

This completes one pattern.

**NB:** Alternatively, the laid cord may be whipped into the loops of the stitches to be missed on the following row. This produces a different-shaped hole.

Variations of this four-hole bud may be made by simply increasing the number of holes that are left in the stitching.

**Variation 1.** Thread one bead for each hole before laying the cord across. Stitch around the bead into the loop immediately above it in the previous row. Repeat with the other rows of beads as shown in the sample.

**Variation 2.** Work surface couronnes in the same sequence as the four-hole bud, taking the threads over one complete row of stitches. Lay three threads and buttonhole over them as for ring picots (chapter 8) worked on the cordonnet.

**Variation 3.** Work long satin-type stitches in the required position – five or six – into the same space between stitches, over two rows.

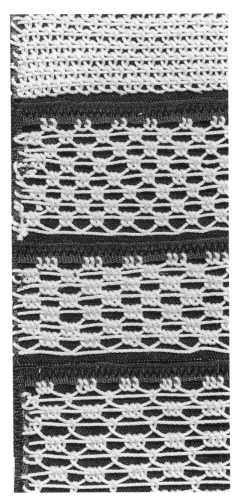

**Fig 123** *Four-hole bud*

**Fig 122** *Illustration of corded stitch and a variation of treble corded Brussels stitch*

**Fig 124** *Illustration of four-hole bud and variations*

*Detail of blue tit showing stripy filling for the chest*

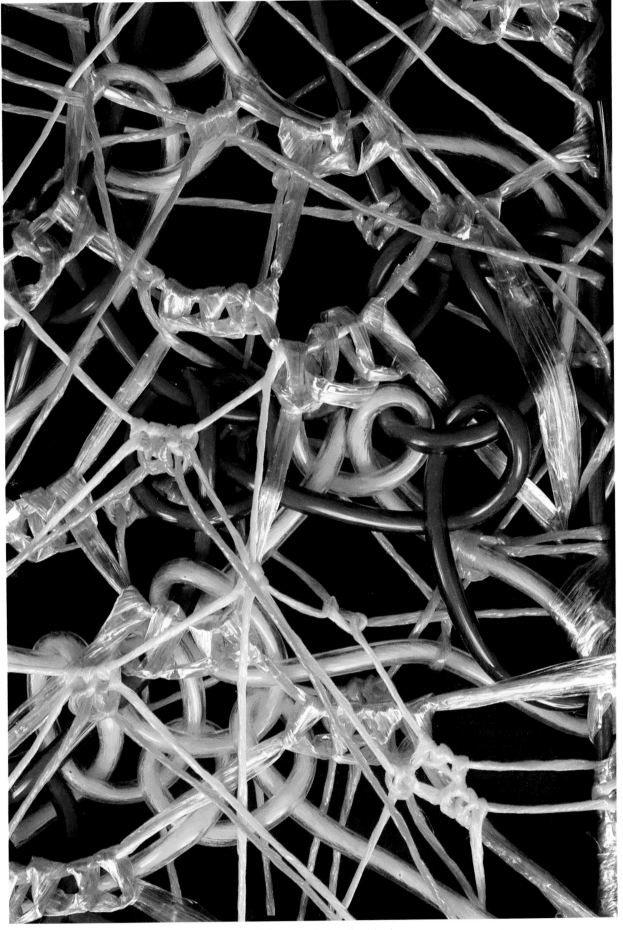

*Layered stitches using plastic raffia and nylon washing line (Ros Hills)*

**Fig 125** *A flower from a Burano copy of a piece of Flemish needlelace, showing a wheel with Point d'Espagne stitches and four-hole bud in the centre (**NB:** the laid cord is whipped in some places and not in others)*

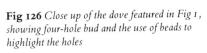

*Silk waistcoat with point de gaze style flower and leaves (Pat Gibson, 1983)*

*Another point de gaze style flower (Pat Gibson, 1986) 5cm × 5cm*

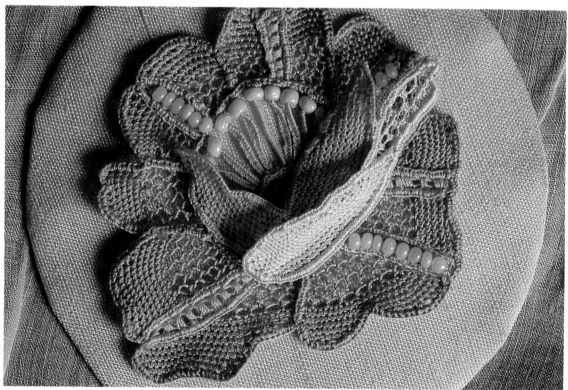

Blue Mountain *grid pattern (Ros Hills)*
*8cm × 6cm*

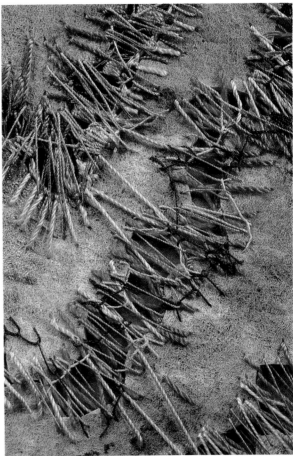

*Random insertion stitchery between hand-dyed*
*vilene sections (Ros Hills)*

**Fig 127** *Cushion. Enlarged point de gaze flower*
*and leaves taken from an old piece of needlelace.*
*Worked in Knox's Linen thread No. 3*
*(Pat Gibson, 1986). 32 cm × 27 cm*

## Corded stitch

A fine degree of shading of the colours you use can be obtained by using the corded stitch. By using thread of more than one colour in your needle you can obtain an all-over shaded effect. The threads could also vary in thickness.

Shading can also be achieved by using two needles, putting the laid thread down as one colour and then stitching over it with another colour, spacing your stitches so that the laid thread may just be glimpsed.

When changing from one colour to another, begin with at least four strands of thread of the first colour. Where you want the shade to start to change, take out one strand of your original colour and replace it with one strand of the new colour. Make two or three rows with this, then remove another strand of your original colour, replacing it with the new colour. Continue in this way until all the old colour has been eliminated.

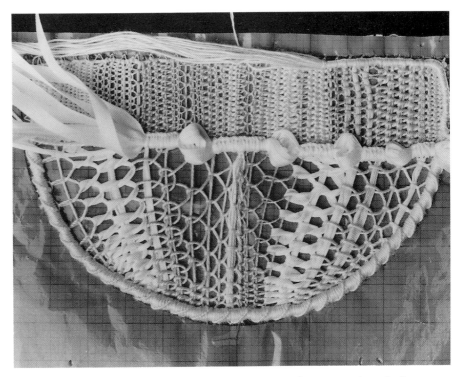

**Fig 128** *Work in progress. One side of a purse using cotton and linen thread with fine silk knitting ribbon (Ros Hills, 1988)*

## Fanned corded stitch

To fill a triangular shape, fan the corded stitch in the following way.

1. Make a row of buttonhole stitches starting in the corner of the triangle, keeping the stitches close together to start with.

2. Whip further down the cordonnet to compensate for the shape, as shown in Fig 129.

3. Take back the working thread to the corner and make the first buttonhole stitch of the second row into the second loop on the first row of stitches. Keep the tension fairly loose as you work so that the stitches can easily become larger towards the outer edge of the shape.

4. Take back the working thread and put the first stitch of the third row into the third loop of the second row. By staggering the start of the rows in this way, you will avoid too much bunching up in the corner of the fan shape.

5. Continue with as many rows as are necessary to fill the space. Use your discretion when selecting the exact starting point of each row, i.e. stagger the stitches backwards and forwards as you work!

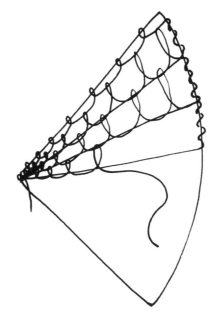

**Fig 129** *Fanned corded stitch*

*A landscape worked by Pat Gibson under the
'tuition' of her co-author at a workshop in Great
Missenden 1987, featuring some of the techniques
described in the 'contemporary' sections of this book*

## Point de Valencienne (variations: corded and beaded)

These are variations of the point de Valencienne from chapter 1, but with a cord laid so that all stitches are worked from the same direction. It is necessary to whip the cord through the loops that will be left without stitches on the next row. In order to whip the correct stitches, it is necessary to calculate where they will appear before commencing the row. The whipping may be omitted, but this means that the resulting hole is not so clear.

The other variation (see Fig 131) has beads threaded on the cord before laying it across. Whipping is not necessary in this case, but the number of beads must be counted carefully before threading. They are then stitched around into the appropriate loop above, as the work progresses across the row.

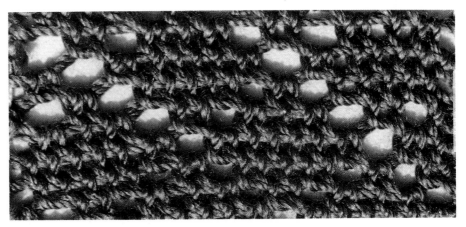

**Fig 130** *Point de Valencienne, corded*

**Fig 131** *Point de Valencienne, beaded*

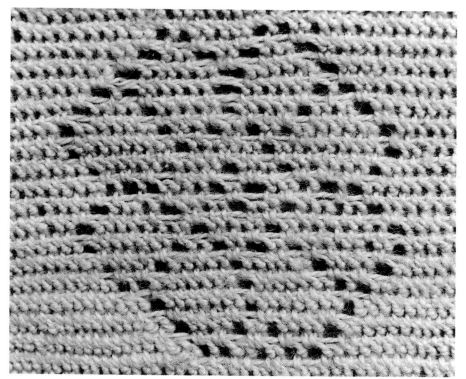

**Fig 132** *Hollie point. A simplified sample to try out the principles. The finished appearance would be improved if the laid cord is whipped on the return, into each loop that will form a hole on the following row. As one loop is missed to produce the*

*hole (this is the design, everything else is solid stitchery), it is impossible to work vertical holes without them becoming larger, so a design should avoid this feature if at all possible*

**Fig 133** *Point d'Anvers – corded variation*

## Point de Turque

This stitch is useful for filling quite large areas, but tends to pack together closely while working. Once the stitch is pulled down and fastened, the true effect can be appreciated.

**Row 1.** Work a loop stitch into the cordonnet, lay the thread from left to right over and under the needle. Pull up fairly tightly. Work in this manner to the end of the row.

**Row 2.** Lay the thread back just beneath the loops of the previous row. Repeat the stitch of row 1 taking up the loops and the laid cord.

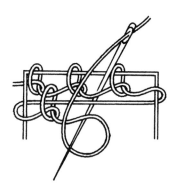

**Fig 134** *Point de Turque*

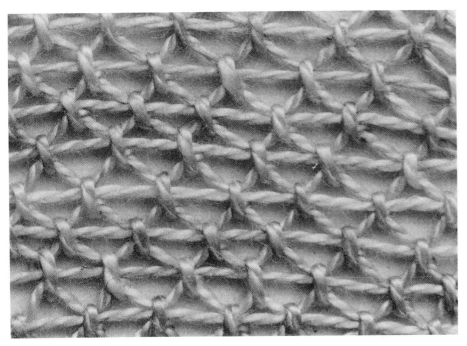

**Fig 135** *Point de Turque*

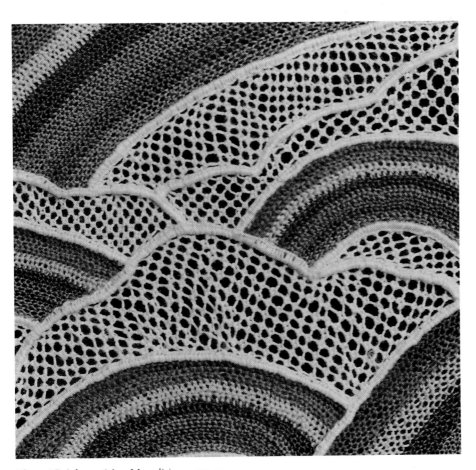

**Fig 136** Rainbows *(Ann Margolis). 9 cm × 7 cm*

**Fig 137** *Decorated point de Valencienne. Decorate this stitch with buttonhole rings, whipped holes and metallic thread passed through the holes to show through*

**Fig 138a** Cottage garden. *Interpret this garden scene using only corded stitch with one or two of the flower areas as decorated point de Valencienne, using more texture in the foreground than in the sky*
**Fig 138b** Rolling Hills or Wavescape. *This line drawing could be any landscape you choose. Develop it as green patchwork fields or as undulating waves. Try using corded stitch with beads in varying degrees of density*

**Fig 139** Fishes – Sardines *(Cynthia Sherwood, 1987)* Fish swimming *(Maureen O'Dwyer, 1987)*

## Leaf veining

It is often necessary to produce a shading change or a vein in a piece of work. There are a number of ways of representing this feature in needlelace. The instructions that follow give only a few of these, worked here into single corded stitch. It is up to the worker to experiment with other ways and to study other pieces of work for further inspiration.

Work single corded stitch to within one row of the desired position of the vein.

1. **To insert a row of beads** (Fig 140)
Thread the beads on the cord that will be laid back. Make sure there are sufficient to fill the space totally, then remove the last three or four beads, depending upon their size (it will be appreciated that it is difficult to give an exact figure because of the differing size of beads, threads and the tension of the worker).
Fasten the cord into the cordonnet. Work back with a row of loop stitches into each loop of the previous row, working around a bead each time to hold it in place. Lay the cord back and continue with single corded stitch until the area is complete.

2. **Point d'Espagne** (Fig 140)
Work as for combination stitch 3a in chapter 2.

3. **Ardenza bar** (Fig 141)
Complete the leaf with single corded stitch, then work Ardenza stitch along the required position of the vein, either laying an extra cord or not as is required. It is possible to work this stitch in a different colour or shade.

4. **Half-couronnes** (Fig 141)
See chapter 8 for the instructions for working these couronnes.

5. **Bar cluster** (Fig 141)
It will be necessary to fill the leaf shape working from both directions in order to leave a parallel space where the vein is required.
Work bar cluster stitch as shown in chapter 7.

6. **Point d'Angleterre** (Fig 140)
Work the leaf filling as for the bar cluster, giving a parallel space in which to work the grid for the Point d'Angleterre wheels. It will be noted that these are only worked over four threads crossing, rather than a grid of eight.

## Corded pyramid stitch variation

This stitch gives an interesting change of texture because the pyramids (or blocks of stitches) fall underneath one another instead of in a staggered formation.

Begin the stitch with a foundation row of spaced loop stitches – each loop to hold six (if smaller triangles are required then four stitches – the number must be even).

Lay back the thread from right to left.
**Row 1.** Work three stitches into the long loops on either side of the stitch in the foundation row. Return with the laid thread.

**Row 2.** Work one stitch on each loop (five stitches) to the end of the row. Return with the laid thread but whip it once around the loop between the blocks of stitches.

**Row 3.** Work as for row 2, but decreasing the number of stitches. Continue in this manner until only one stitch remains to be worked at the apex of the triangle.

Continue the pattern from row 1.

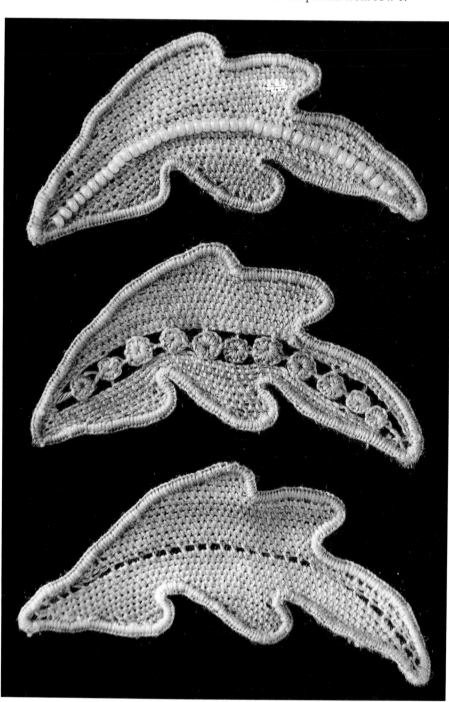

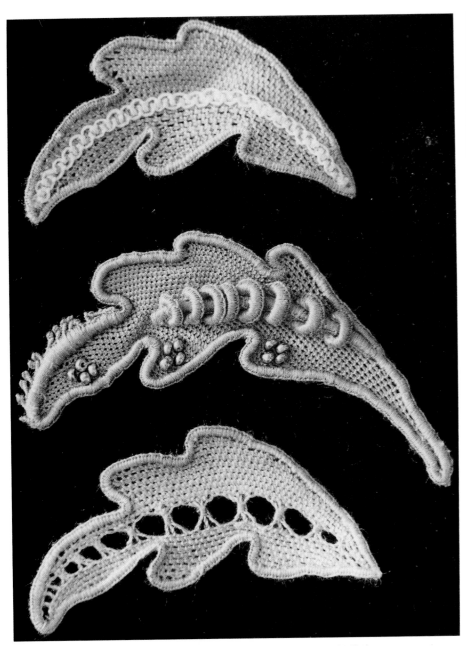

**Fig 142** *Corded pyramid variation (see Fig 48 for directions)*

**Fig 141** *Illustration of different ways to create a vein: Ardenza bar, half couronnes, bar cluster*

**Fig 140** *Illustration of different ways to create a vein: beads, point d'Angleterre, point d'Espagne*

## Flame stitch

To create areas of colour on the front of
close corded stitch, thread a needle with
your extra colour and carry it with the
working thread, bringing the extra colour
up to make a stitch where you want it,
then taking the colour to the side of the
space under the cordonnet, and back
across the space to await use again.

The working thread then continues
across the row, making more stitches in
the ground colour but only picking up its
own laid thread (not the laid thread of the
contrast colour). This stitch will produce
'floating' threads on the back of the work.

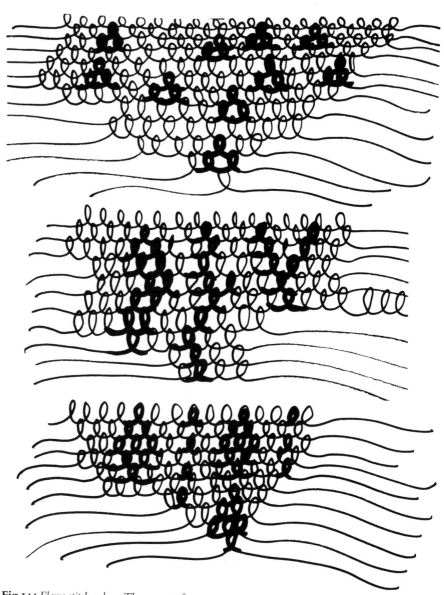

**Fig 143** *Flame stitch. The 'thin' thread only picks
up 'thin' loops and laid threads. The 'thick' thread
only picks up 'thick' loops and laid threads*

**Fig 144** *Flame stitch a, b, c. Three ways of
creating areas of colour change using the flame stitch
method. (**NB:** to avoid confusion these diagrams do
not show the laid threads)*

**Fig 145** *Flame stitch. Knitting yarn and metallic thread*

**Fig 146** *Leaf border pattern. Stitch in shades of green from pale yellowish greens through to deep emeralds*

## Block and bar cluster

Work a foundation row of groups of four loop stitches, leaving space between for four stitches. Lay the thread back from right to left, whipping twice in the spaces.

**Row 1.** Work one stitch into each loop of the first block of four (three stitches), four into the long loop, one into each of the next block of four (ten stitches in all); to the end of the row.

Lay back the thread whipping the long loops twice.

**Row 2.** Miss the first loop of the block of ten, work one into each of the next seven stitches, miss the last loop. Continue in this manner to the end.

Lay the thread back as in row 1.

**Row 3.** Work two stitches before the block, one into each loop of the block, and two into the loop at the end (ten stitches).

Lay back the thread, whip the long loop and the centre three stitches of the block of ten.

**Row 4.** Work blocks of four as in the foundation row, as follows:

Work one stitch into each of the last three of the block of ten, one stitch into the long loop, gather together all the long loops of the previous four rows and work two buttonhole stitches over them (as in bar cluster, chapter 7); one stitch into the loop and one into each of the next three. Continue to the end of the row. Lay the thread back as in row 1.

Continue the pattern from row 1, arranging blocks under bar clusters as in Fig 147.

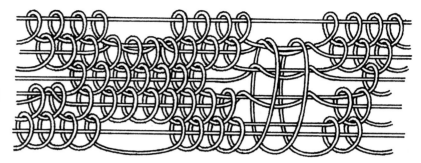

**Fig 147** *Block and bar cluster*

**Fig 148** *Block and bar cluster*

## Blossom stitch

Work a foundation row of groups of four stitches, leaving space between for four stitches. Whip back through the long loops and the centre loop of the block of four.

**Row 1.** Work five stitches into the long loop and one twisted (point d'Espagne) stitch into the centre whipped loop. Continue to the end.

Whip back, leaving the cord lying under the blocks of stitches, but whip on either side of the twisted stitch.

**Row 2.** One stitch into each loop of the block of five (four stitches), one point d'Espagne into the base of that stitch of the previous row, continue to the end.

Whip back as for the foundation row.

**Row 3.** Work one point d'Espagne into the centre of the block of four, three stitches into the loop to the left of the twisted stitch, two to the right (forming block of five), continue to the end.

Whip back as for row 1.

**Row 4.** One point d'Espagne stitch into the base of that stitch on the previous row, four into the block of five, and continue to the end.

Repeat rows 3 and 4 to continue the pattern.

**Fig 149** *Blossom stitch*

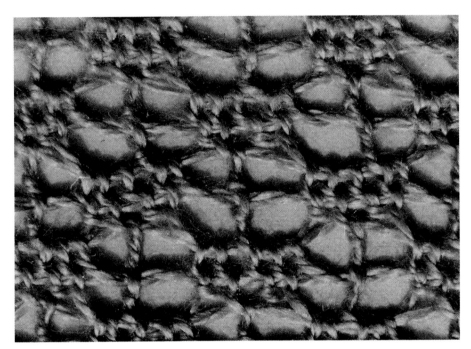

**Fig 150** *Blossom stitch*

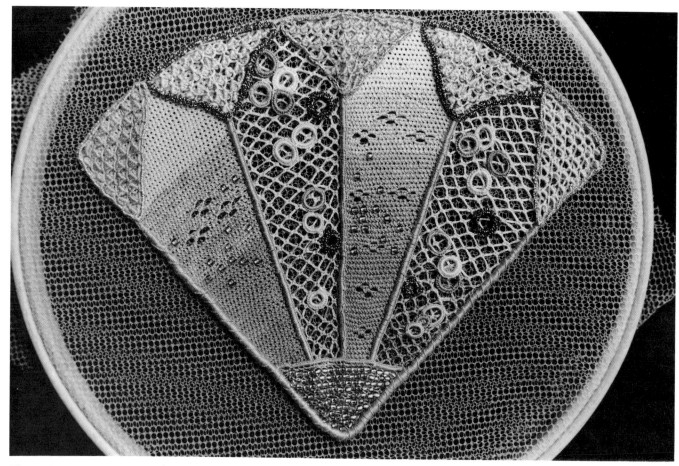

**Fig 151** *Purse in progress (Joan Hake, 1986)*

**Fig 152** Birds of a feather, *a design to work*

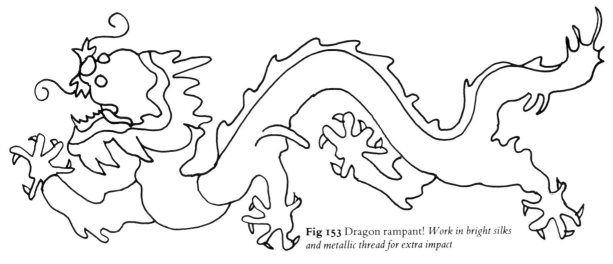

**Fig 153** Dragon rampant! *Work in bright silks and metallic thread for extra impact*

**Fig 154** Stumpwork bird. *The design for this piece was inspired by stumpwork in the Burrell Collection in Glasgow (Barbara Hirst, 1987)*

**Fig 155** The Lady of Shallot. '. . . *on either side the river lie, long fields of barley and of rye . . .*' *Part of a series of seven pieces depicting scenes from* The Lady of Shallot, *designed and worked by Ros Hills, 1987. Approx 6cm square*

# CHAPTER FIVE

# Grids

## Maltese filling

**Stage 1.** Lay in threads as shown. Knot stitch alternate groups of three.

**Stage 2.** Lay diagonals through remaining sections. Knot stitch '16' crossing.

**Stage 3.** Weave on groups of three threads tapering to a point at '16' crossing

**Stage 4.** Run thread through weaving and out to form a third leg of the diagonal crossing, weave on these three and continue across to form the fourth diagonal. Complete as shown in Fig 157.

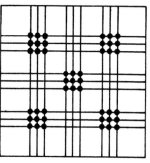

*stage 1*

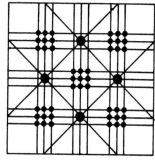

*stage 2*

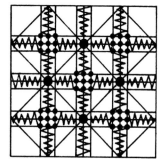

*stage 3*

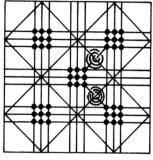

*stage 4*

**Fig 156** *Maltese filling, stage 1*
*stage 2*
*stage 3*
*stage 4*

**Fig 157** *Maltese filling*

# Marguerite filling (or buttonhole star)

It is worth studying the illustration of this stitch (Fig 159) before commencing. Each star occupies nine squares of mesh, which may be sufficient in itself to fill the required area.

Lay in the horizontal and vertical rays approximately 6mm apart. Knot stitch at all points of crossing. Decide whereabouts the 'stars' are required before commencing filling. They may be worked either as in the illustration or in straight lines. The empty squares may also be filled with a woven wheel, as is the centre of the square.

1. Attach the working thread to the top left-hand corner of the centre square. Make a buttonhole stitch on the outer edge of the square, pass the needle under the lower edge and back to the outer edge for the next buttonhole stitch. Refer to the enlarged diagram (Fig 158) for the formation of the stitch and weaving.

   Continue working until the weaving reaches the centre of the lower edge. Run the needle through these loops back to the top left-hand corner, then work as before on the next square.

2. Continue to fill all the squares around the centre in this manner.

3. When all the weaving is complete, lay in the diagonal threads through the centre of the stars.

4. Work a woven wheel at the point of crossing, then whip along the thread to the next star.

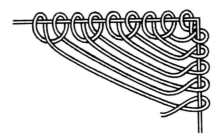

**Fig 158** *Marguerite filling, showing the method of weaving*

**Fig 159** *Marguerite filling*

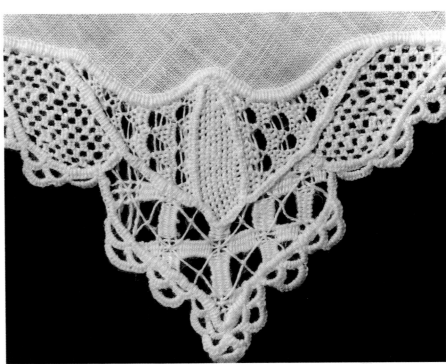

**Fig 160** *Handkerchief corner featuring: pyramid stitch, double Brussels stitch, single corded Brussels stitch, Maltese filling variation (Pat Gibson, 1982)*

**Fig 161** *Wrapped perspex with random stitching*
*(Ros Hills)*

**Fig 162** *Point de reprise – needleweaving with different textured threads*

grids used for
purse design

using gold stranded thread

using fine ribbon
as a base
then weaving with
gold stranded thread.

**Fig 163** *Line drawings of grids used for purse design using stranded gold thread and fine ribbon as a base, with the gold thread as a weaver*

## Tudor rose

A square mesh filling suitable for a fairly large area.

1. Lay cords at right angles approximately 6mm apart, fastening into the cordonnet each time.
2. Cross the alternate threads diagonally with a double thread.
3. Cross again diagonally in the opposite direction. Return to create a double thread, knotting where twelve threads cross.
4. From the centre of one group of twelve threads, weave over three threads, taking one of a pair from a diagonal, a single thread and one from the next adjacent pair. Weave halfway to the centre of a single thread crossing, take the needle through the weaving back to the centre and repeat on three more groups of three threads making four petals.
5. Whip along to the next group of twelve. Repeat step 4 until the area is filled.
6. Make a knot stitch, if wished, where four single threads cross, before proceeding to the next flower.

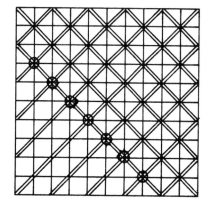

**Fig 164** *Tudor Rose mesh*

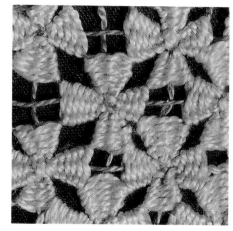

**Fig 165** *Tudor Rose*

## Picot strand

1. Divide the area to be filled by laying threads across the space in groups of four. Each group should be approximately 1 cm apart, the rays 3 mm apart.
2. Cross these threads at right angles in the same manner. Knot the rays where they all cross.
3. Weave on two strands nine times. Take the thread back into the sixth weaving, work a buttonhole stitch, then five more stitches into the loop to form a picot. Weave six more times. This should fill the strands.
   Repeat on the next two strands until all the strands are filled.

   For the position of the picots see Fig 166.

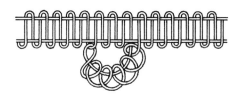

**Fig 166** *Picot strand*

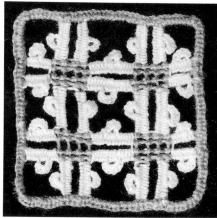

**Fig 167** *Picot strand*

## Darned corners

Divide the areas as for Marguerite filling. The completed design once again occupies nine squares of mesh.

1. Lay in a diagonal thread across the four outer squares (see Fig 168).
2. It is now possible to darn over four bars of the foundation threads and one diagonal thread.
3. When the darning reaches the half-way point of the squares, whip along to the next corner and repeat.
4. When all the corners are complete, work point d'Espagne stitches (chapter 2) around the centre, spaced as in the illustration, then whip the loops.

**Fig 168** *Darned corners*

## Point d'Angleterre

1. Lay double threads across the space as shown in Fig 169, weaving them at the point of crossing.
   Each ring should start and finish at this point.
2. Join in a thread at an eight-point crossing. Weave four or five times around this point; do not pull the weaving too tightly.
3. Put the needle into the centre and buttonhole over the weavings around the circle.
4. To finish this thread, run it through the buttonhole stitches at the back and cut off.
   Rejoin the thread at the next eight-point crossing and repeat until the crossings are complete.

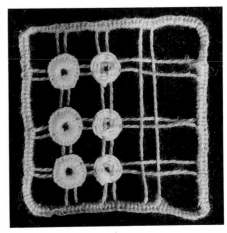

**Fig 169** *Point d'Angleterre*

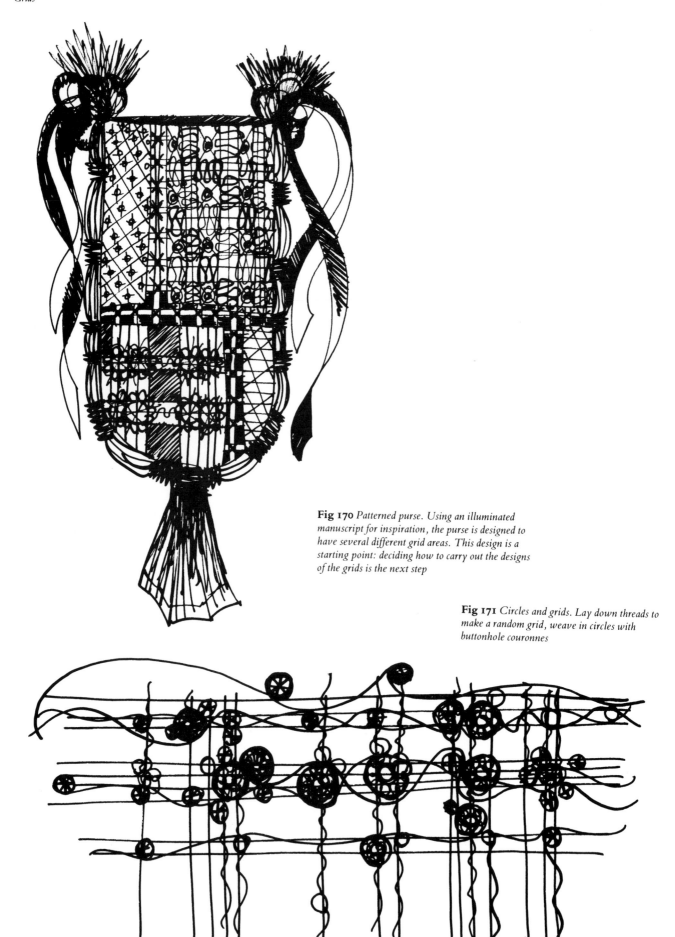

**Fig 170** *Patterned purse. Using an illuminated manuscript for inspiration, the purse is designed to have several different grid areas. This design is a starting point: deciding how to carry out the designs of the grids is the next step*

**Fig 171** *Circles and grids. Lay down threads to make a random grid, weave in circles with buttonhole couronnes*

**Fig 172** Smartie. *Grid with couronnes*

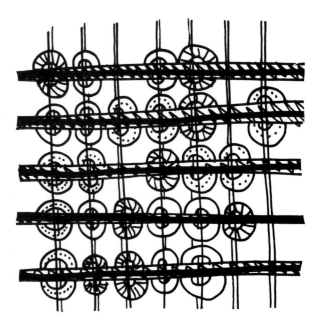

**Fig 173** *Laid grid with circles of different colours*

## Brugge filling

This is a square mesh filling worked
without first laying the mesh. It is made
up as the stitch progresses.

**Row 1.** Lay a thread from one side to the
other of the space to be filled. Knot stitch
into the cordonnet. Make a buttonhole
stitch immediately below this knot stitch.

**Row 2.** Calculate from the space
available where the intersections in the
mesh will occur. Half-way between the
cordonnet and the point of crossing, work
a buttonhole stitch.

At the intersection work two single point
de Venise (chapter 3). Work another
buttonhole stitch at the next half-way
point.

Continue across the laid thread in this
manner.

At the edge, whip down the cordonnet to
correspond with the intersection space of
the first row.

Continue to fill the space, repeating rows
1 and 2.

**Row 3.** To cross the threads at right
angles, fasten the thread to the cordonnet
in line with the first group of two point
de Venise. Take the thread through the
centre of these stitches, continue to the
opposite edge and knot stitch.

**Row 4.** Work back making a buttonhole
stitch on to this thread at the half-way
point.

At the intersections, weave around the
threads to form a wheel. Continue along
the thread in this manner to the other side.
Whip along the cordonnet to the next
point of intersection and repeat rows 3
and 4 until all the crossings are complete.

**Fig 174a** *Brugge filling, stage 1*

**Fig 174b** *Brugge filling, stage 2*

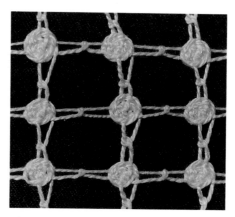

**Fig 175** *Brugge filling*

## Spider wheel filling (or raised point d'Angleterre)

1. Lay in the right angle crossings first.
2. Lay in the diagonal crossings in one direction.
3. Lay in the other diagonal threads, working a knot stitch at an eight-point crossing.
4. Work a spider (see chapter 6) on each group of eight.

## Woven wheel filling

1. Lay in equidistant rays in both directions.
2. Lay in a diagonal through all the squares in one direction only. (This should give six spokes at the point of crossing.)
3. Begin laying the diagonal rays in the opposite direction.
   On reaching the first point of crossing it is now possible to work a woven wheel over seven rays. After three or four rounds, thread the needle through the weaving in order to form the eighth spoke.
   Continue to the next point of crossing.

   Proceed through all points, whip the thread along the cordonnet to the next square and repeat.

## Woven wheel and block filling (or Rose point lace stitch)

1. Lay in equidistant rays in both directions.
   Work a knot stitch at all points of crossing.
2. Fill all alternate squares with single Brussels stitch.
   **NB:** In order to achieve a better tension it may be advisable to insert a few couching stitches over the rays before commencing to fill the squares.
3. Cross the open squares diagonally in both directions. Weave at the centre of these points two or three times. The weaving may be done over three threads while laying in the second set of diagonals. Take the weaving thread across as the fourth diagonal (Fig 178b).

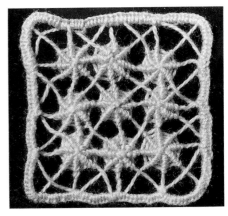

**Fig 176** *Spider wheel filling, or raised point d'Angleterre*

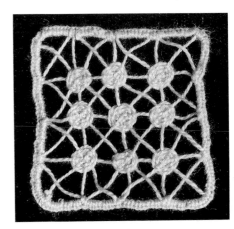

**Fig 177** *Woven wheel filling*

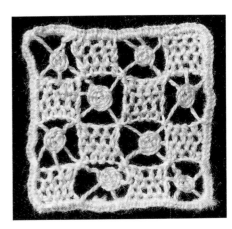

**Fig 178** *Woven wheel and block filling, or rose point lace stitch*

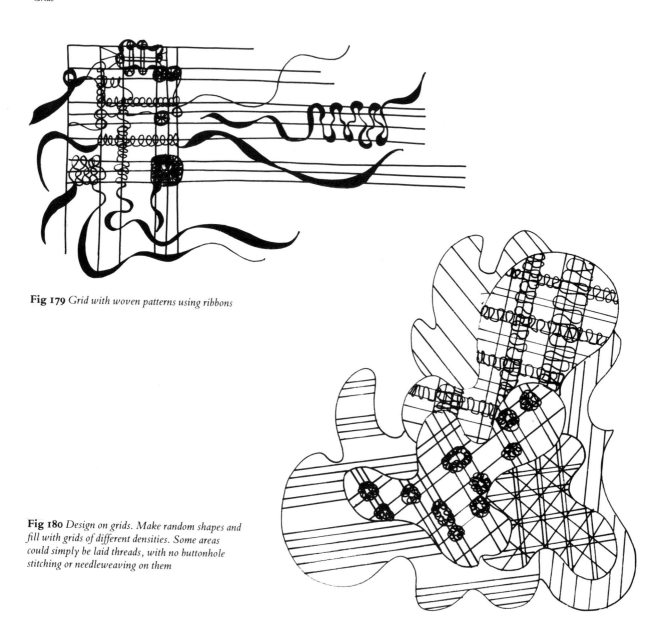

**Fig 179** *Grid with woven patterns using ribbons*

**Fig 180** *Design on grids. Make random shapes and fill with grids of different densities. Some areas could simply be laid threads, with no buttonhole stitching or needleweaving on them*

**Fig 181** Box *(Angela White, 1987)*

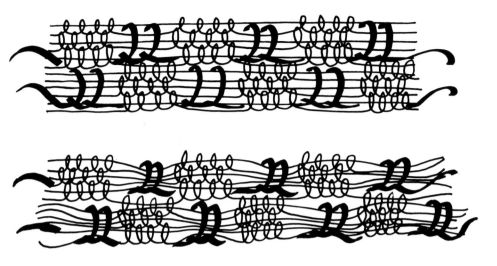

**Fig 182** *Block and bar. A corded stitch giving a grid appearance*

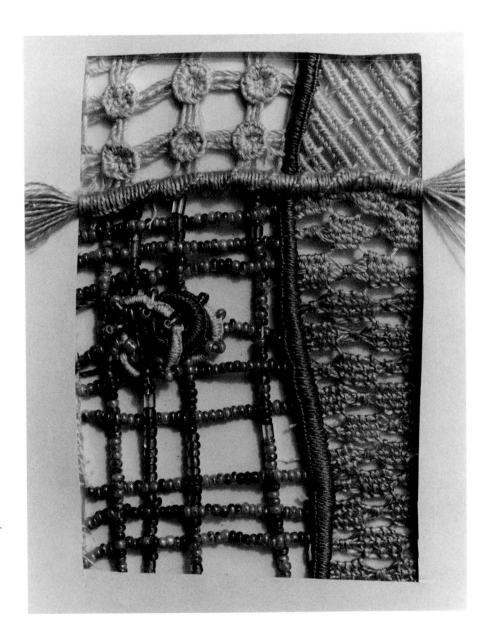

**Fig 183** *Grid sampler, showing top left a grid of laid threads with buttonhole rings.*
*Top right – a grid of buttonhole bars and single threads.*
*Bottom left – beaded laid threads with beaded couronnes for decoration*
*Bottom right – block and bar*

## Brussels courounne ground

1. Divide the area to be filled into equal-sized squares.
2. Couch the horizontal and vertical lines with a double thread.
3. Divide these squares in half in both directions using double thread.
4. Lay in the diagonals in both directions. Knot stitch at all the points of crossing except in the centre of the squares where eight double threads cross.
5. Outline both sides of the couched squares as shown in Fig 184 with any of the following stitches: single Brussels, point d'Espagne or Ardenza bar.
6. Weave several times in the centre of the squares around all the threads, then buttonhole stitch the weaving, making a single picot (chapter 8), in the space between each ray.
7. The couronne at the corners of the squares was made on a ring stick and added later.

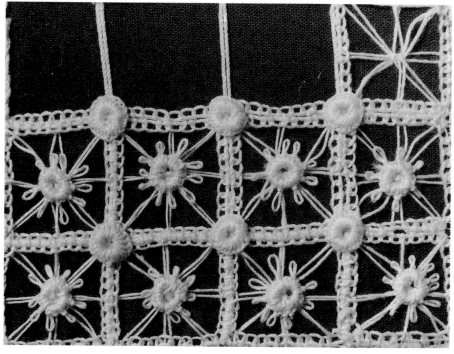

**Fig 184** *Brussels couronne ground*

## Ghost stitch

Lay vertical and horizontal threads across the whole area, spacing them equally to produce squares. It may be worth measuring the area and marking it out accurately first.

Knot stitch (Fig 89) at all the points of crossing.

1. Fasten the working thread to the side cordonnet and work evenly-spaced loop stitches into the centre of each square.
2. It may be easier at this point to turn the work upside down. Return along the row, working loops into the next row of net, but also going over the previous loop and behind the ray (see Fig 185).

Continue to fill the whole area in this manner.

Finally, weave around each point of crossing in the centre of the circles, whipping along the ray to the next circle. (Alternatively, leave these centres open as shown by part of the illustration.)

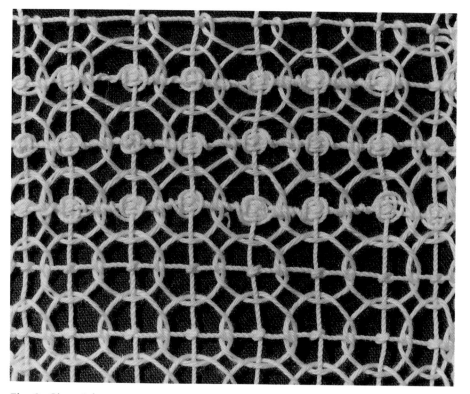

**Fig 185** *Ghost stitch*

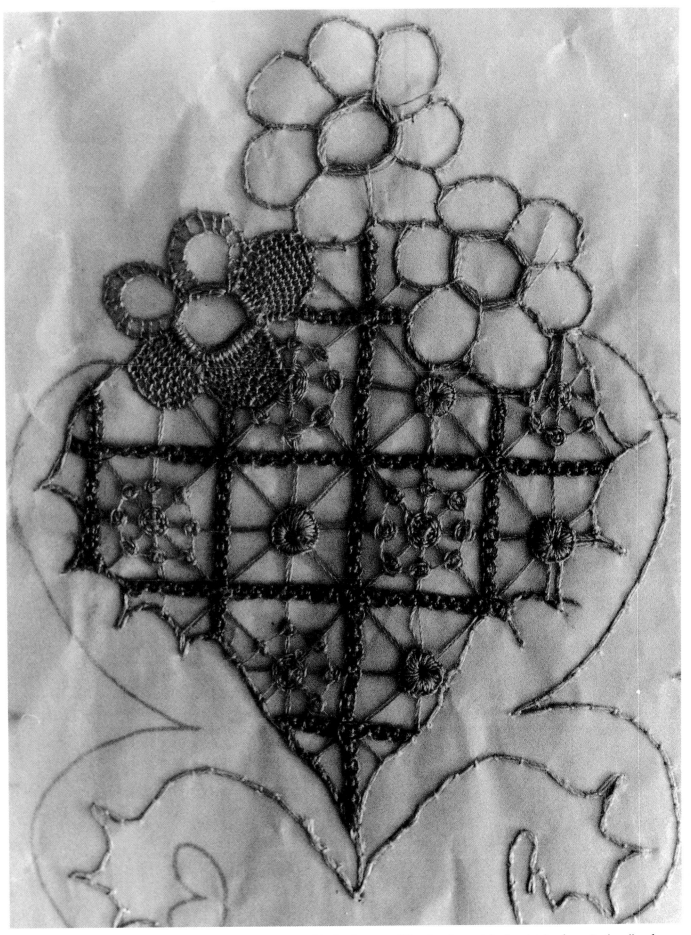

**Fig 186** *Woven wheel and couronne filling, found on a piece of old lace. The work is still in progress, and the shape is taken from a Bertha collar of Burano needlelace (Pat Gibson, 1988)*

## Woven wheel and couronne filling (Fig 186)

1. Couch squares approximately 1.5 cm apart in both directions.
2. Lay double diagonal threads through all the squares in both directions.
3. Cross the square at right angles, also with double thread. (In order to lay a double thread, work across the space with a single thread, then return, laying the second thread very close to the first.)
4. Join all eight double rays at the centre with a knot stitch.
5. In alternating squares, weave around these five or six times. (If one of the double threads is separated and taken as a ninth ray, then weaving becomes much easier. If this is not done, it will be necessary to go under two rays on every round.)
6. Whip along one ray half-way to the outer edge of the square. Knot stitch. Cross to the next ray. Knot stitch. Weave four times over these threads. Bring the needle up through the centre of the weaving, stretch across to the next ray and knot stitch.
7. Work another woven wheel on these three rays just formed. Continue on all eight rays in this manner. This forms a point d'Angleterre wheel.
8. The centre of the alternate squares is filled with a woven and buttonholed wheel. Find the centre after weaving three or four times and buttonhole around the wheel to cover all the weaving.
9. To complete the design, use Ardenza stitch or point d'Espagne along each edge of all the squares.

**Fig 187** *Three abstract designs to work in close stitchery. Leave spaces in the stitchery for extra interest: the lace should be 'holey'*

**Fig 188** Wheels and windmills. *Lay a foundation grid with some diagonals, then needleweave at random windmills and wheels*

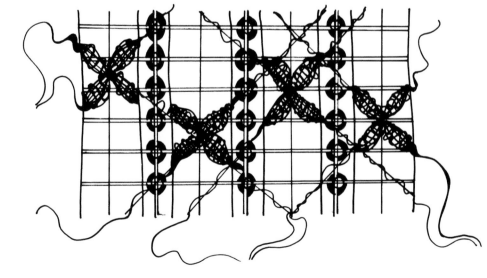

**Fig 189** Egyptian visit. *These striking plant shapes would look wonderful as a decoration on an evening jacket. Make the circles in gold metallic couronnes and the leaf shapes in purples and cerise tints, all in a close corded stitch*

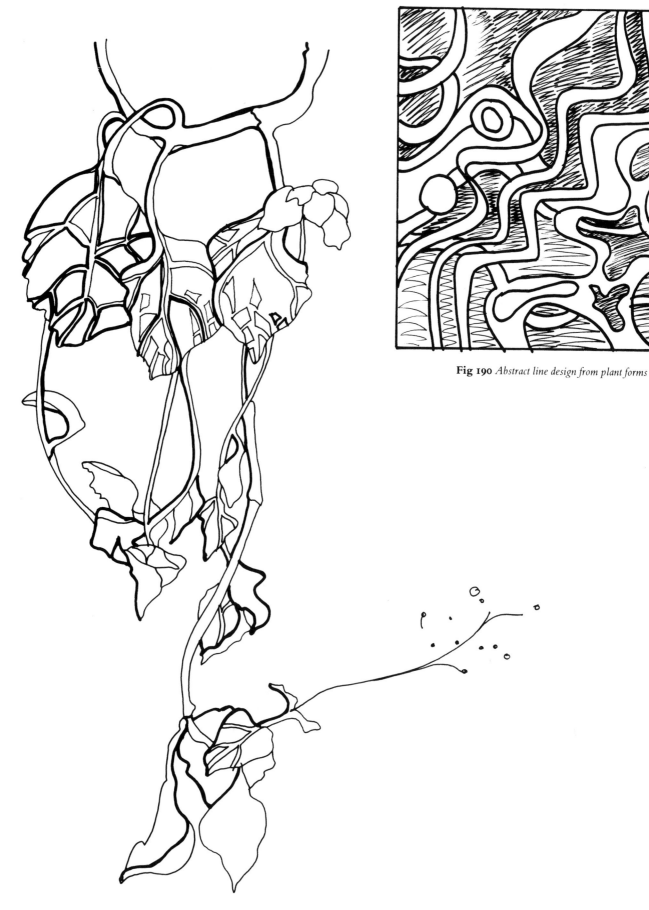

**Fig 190** *Abstract line design from plant forms*

**Fig 191** *Leaf trail*

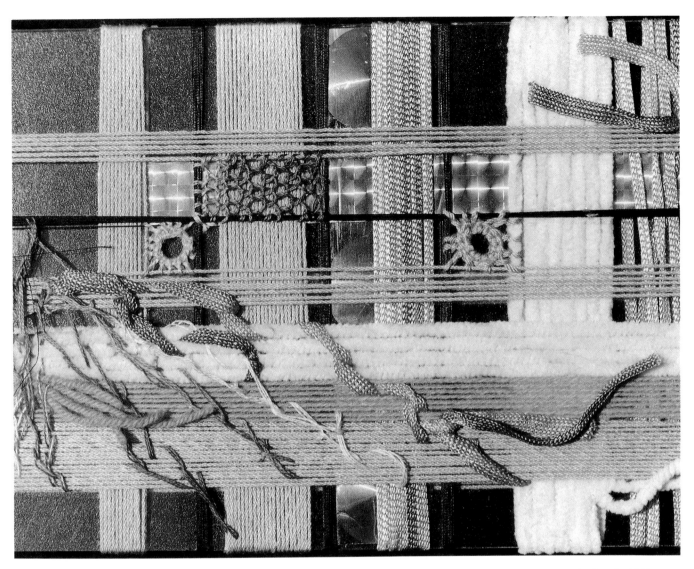

**Fig 192** *Perspex, wrapped and stitched (Eileen Plumbridge)*

# CHAPTER SIX

# Filling a circle

Circles or wheels are often used in traditional lace designs. They form focal points, they fill in small spaces, they enhance and embellish in the form of extra decoration. In contemporary design, circles may also be used as a basis for a piece of work. Make use of bought metal, wood or plastic circles on which to work.

Run circles through a design and fill the centres with laid thread, beads, sequins, ribbons or metallic threads. Having laid your threads down, you can needleweave or buttonhole stitch between, over and around them. If you are working on a metal ring, it helps to buttonhole stitch around the ring itself so that you can use these stitches as anchorage points for the threads that you might lay in across the circle. Rigid rings may be buttonholed in a wide variety of ways, as the diagrams show.

### A woven wheel

Fig 193 shows how to work a woven wheel, over an even number of rays. For the weaving to alternate it becomes necessary to go under two rays at the end of each round.

### Spider wheel

Fig 194 shows how to work the 'spider' wheel, which accentuates the 'ribs' as it gets progressively larger.

Work over one rib from right to left, taking the needle under two, go back

over the last of these two and under two again. Continue until the desired amount of the circle has been filled.

### Circles

These ideas are for inspiration. There is no right way or wrong way in which to carry them out. Problems encountered in their creation must be solved as they arise, using initiative. You will notice that the threads in the designs extend over the edge of the circles in some cases: this helps to 'free' the rather 'tight' restriction of the circle shape.

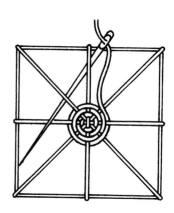

**Fig 193** *Working the woven wheel*

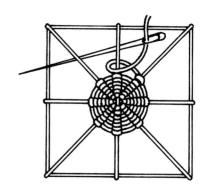

**Fig 194** *Working the spider wheel*

**Fig 195** *An enlarged section from a piece of mid nineteenth-century point de gaze needlelace, featuring wheel fillings, particularly the point d'Angleterre wheel. Notice how the cordonnette buttonholing is evenly spaced, not closely packed as in other needlelaces*

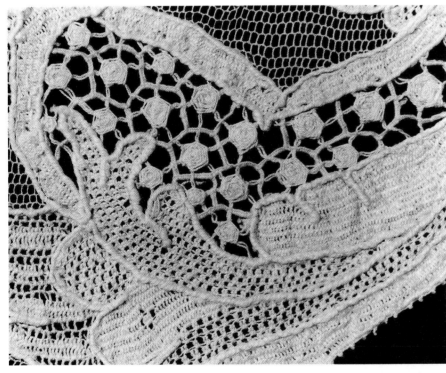

**Fig 196** *From a Bertha collar of nineteenth-century Burano needlelace, featuring point d'Espagne as whipped ground stitch, spider wheel showing the reverse side, and double corded Brussels stitch. Also, the cordonnette is without extra raising, which has been whipped instead of buttonholed*

**Fig 197** *A wheel filling from a piece of Brussels Duchesse mixed lace (property of Pat Gibson). 3 cm × 3.5 cm*

**Fig 198** *Six examples of stitching around a rigid ring: a) with beads, b) in groups of three buttonhole stitches, c) knots on the outside edge, d) with simple picots, e) spiralled buttonhole stitch, f) knot on the inside of the ring*

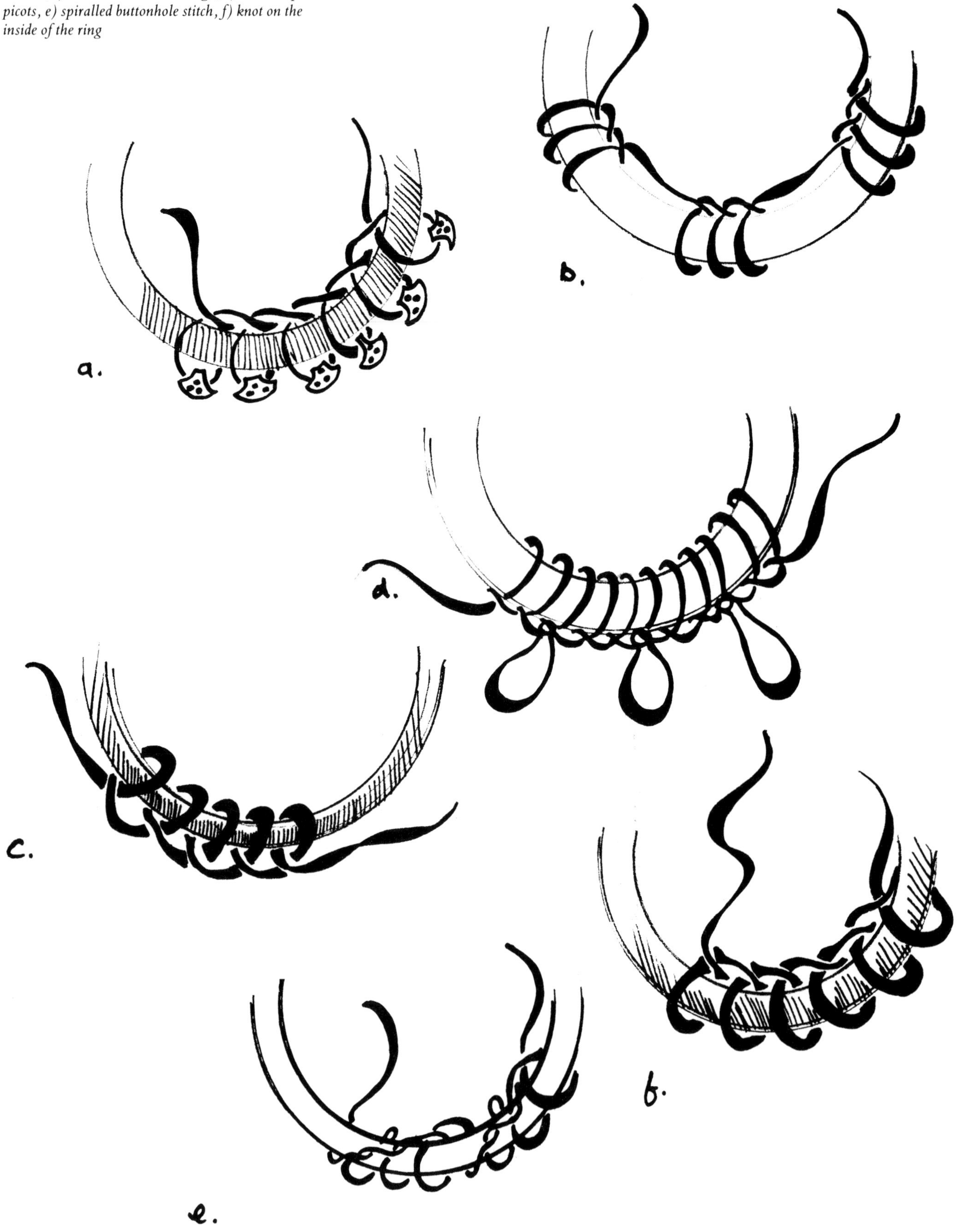

a.

b.

d.

c.

f.

e.

**Fig 199** *Circles. Trace off a circle on to architects'
linen, then couch a rigid ring down and lay in some
crossing threads. Buttonhole stitch in the shaded
areas of the pattern to create fillings. Make several
rings of different sizes and hang together as a mobile*

## Loop stitch star

A simple, yet very effective wheel.

Divide the circular space to be filled either by marking with a pencil, or by eye, into six, seven or eight portions.

**Round 1.** Work a loop stitch pulled up, but not too tightly, joining into the cordonnet at each mark, arriving back at the starting point.

**Round 2.** Work one loop stitch over each loop of the previous round.

**Round 3.** Work one loop stitch over two loops of the previous round.

**Round 4.** Work one loop stitch over three loops of the previous round.

Continue in this manner, working over one more loop after each round until reaching the centre.

The whole area need not be filled.

To join in extra thread or to add a shade change: work the old thread through all the loops to the ouside edge and fasten off. Join in a new length and thread through to come out at the same position, Continue until the area is completely filled or until the desired amount has been reached.

## Open triangles

Lay an even or an odd number of rays within the circular shape. Knot stitch at the centre, then work a spider over approximately one third of the space.

Use the last of these rounds as a foundation for the next sequence of stitches.

Work three buttonhole stitches into the space between two rays, take the thread back and work a buttonhole stitch between the first two of these stitches.

Take the working thread to the outer edge of the circle at the point where it is crossed by a ray; knot stitch.

Cross to the next segment, knot stitch as shown in Fig 89, and continue working groups of buttonhole stitches, forming open triangles in the spaces, until all the segments are complete.

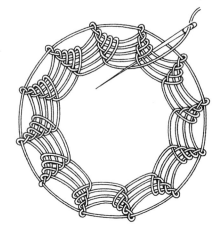

**Fig 200** *Loop stitch star*

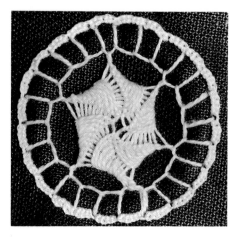

**Fig 201** *Loop stitch star*

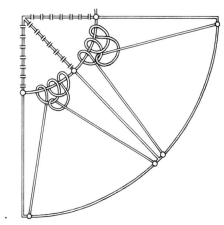

**Fig 202** *Open triangles*

**Fig 203** *Open triangles*

# Scallop shell wheel

In the circular shape lay twelve rays, knotting in the centre.

**Stage 1.** Work a wheel, forward under two, back over one, for one third of the space (a spider).

**Stage 2.** Weave around three times (it is necessary to go under two on each round to alternate the weaving).

**Stage 2a.** On these woven threads work close buttonhole stitches, the same number between each ray.

**Stage 3.** Work a buttonhole stitch into the first group of stitches in Stage 2a, then loop across to the last stitch, behind the ray to the first in the next group; continue around each section in this manner.

**Stage 3a.** Work buttonhole stitches on these loops, making a series of small scallops.

**Stage 4.** Whip along a ray for one quarter of its length. Work a knot stitch. Continue working around, knotting at each ray. Weave once around the circle.

**Stage 4a.** Buttonhole seven or eight times on these two threads all around each section.

**Stage 5.** Take the thread through the stitch of the last row nearest to the ray that has just been reached, then back to the previous ray. (Do not pull this too tightly.) Make three more loops in this manner (four loops in all) and buttonhole an uneven number forming a scallop. Repeat on all other rays.

Fasten the thread off through the back of the stitches, carefully.

**Stage 6.** Join a new thread to the outside circle, whip along to the centre point of the scallop, work through this centre stitch, and back to the outside. Pull this stitch tightly to raise the scallop in an arc. Continue around all rays. Finish with a buttonhole edging or lay on a cordonnette depending upon the position of the wheel.

**NB:** If the circle to be filled is fairly small, this wheel could be concluded after stage 3a.

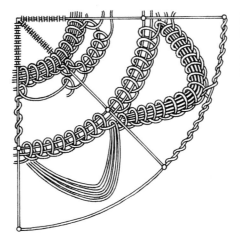

**Fig 204** *Scallop shell wheel*

**Fig 205** *Scallop shell wheel*

**Fig 206** *Enlargement from an early piece of Alençon needlelace featuring wheel fillings, and wheel style insertions, whipped point d'Espagne ground filling and the use of horsehair in the edging picots*

**Fig 207** Threads on a circle *(Ros Hills, 1988)*

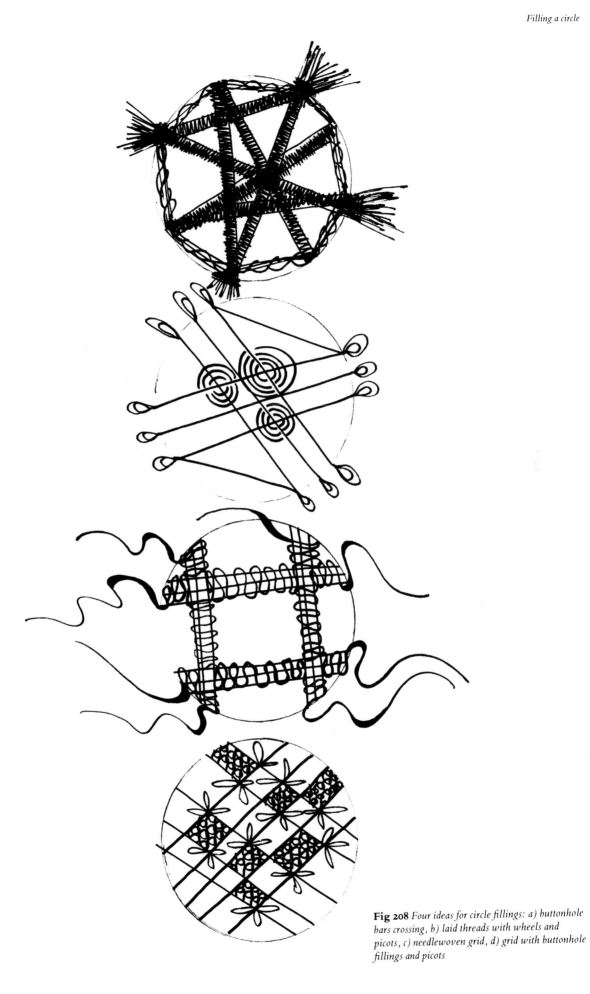

**Fig 208** *Four ideas for circle fillings: a) buttonhole bars crossing, b) laid threads with wheels and picots, c) needlewoven grid, d) grid with buttonhole fillings and picots*

## Pyramid Stitch circle

Couch a small couronne – without the finished buttonholing – into the centre of the circle. Work two rows of loop stitches around the inside of the circle.

**Round 1.** Divide these stiches so that loops are formed with an equal number of stitches between each.

**Round 2.** Work six buttonhole stitches into each long loop.

**Round 3.** Work five buttonhole stitches – one into each loop of the six from the previous row.

Continue working rounds with decreasing numbers of stitches until only one stitch is required.

**Final Round.** Work the stitch into the base of the pyramid, take the needle through the centre couronne and back up to the next pyramid. Continue around all eight in this manner.

After the last stitch, take the thread back to the centre couronne and buttonhole all around it. Fasten off the thread by running it through the back of some of these stitches.

**Fig 210** *Pyramid stitch circle*

**Fig 209** *Sampler of wheel fillings (Pat Gibson, 1988)*

## Spider and woven wheel

Lay in eight rays around the circle. Knot stitch in the centre to bring all the threads together, then work a spider until just less than half the circle has been filled.

Fasten the thread off by carefully feeding it through the back of the loops along a ray to the centre. Join in a new thread on the outer edge, whip half-way along the remainder of a ray, knot stitch. Proceed to the next point of crossing. Knot stitch. Weave three or four times around these three threads so formed, pass the needle through the back of the threads and bring out to form the fourth ray. Continue to the next point of crossing and work another woven wheel in this manner.

Continue around the circle as shown in Fig 211.

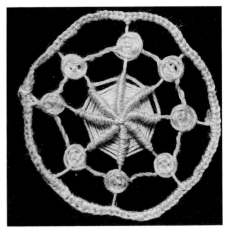

**Fig 211** *Spider and woven wheel*

**Fig 212** *Circle filling from a mid nineteenth-century point de gaze shawl featuring point d'Angleterre filling, woven only, surrounded by couronnes, forming the centre of the flower.*
*45 cm × 238 cm*

**Fig 213** Mobile. *Having made lots of circles,*
*suspend them with ribbon on a bar of metal, wood*
*or perspex. Hang in a window*

**Fig 214** Steering a path. *Inspired by the shapes within car steering wheels, this design could be an exciting piece of lace*

## Pyramid and bar cluster

Divide the circular space into eight equal portions by drawing at right angles through the centre. Then, using a protractor, mark the 45° positions and draw in the diagonal lines.

Draw a small circle around the centre point.

Where the diagonal lines (those drawn at 45°) cut the small circle, draw a straight line to the outside of the circle. This should give four triangles and four parallel areas as shown in the sample (Fig 215).

Work a decreasing number of loop stitches on each round, taking the thread across the space.

As the fourth round proceeds, work two loop stitches over the three bars to form a cluster and continue around the circle. The number of bar cluster groups made up of four strands depends upon the number of stitches in the first round.

**NB:** If the thread is too short, as it inevitably will be, run the needle carefully through an outer edge group of stitches in the pyramid and fasten off at the outside edge of the circle.

Join a new thread in on the same or adjacent row of stitches, so as not to create a ridge.

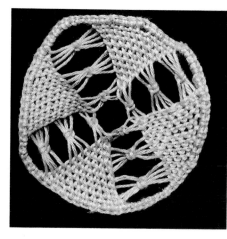

Fig 215 *Pyramid and bar cluster wheel*

## Woven triangles

Couch a second circle inside the main area, approximately two thirds from the centre.

Divide the circle into sixteen equal portions. (It may be a good idea to mark these points, particularly where they cross the inner circle.) Work two rows of loop stitches or point d'Espagne around the inside of the circle.

Whip through all the loops.

Lay in the threads for the woven triangles.

Join a thread to the inside couched circles where one ray would cross. Link it through a stitch on the outer circle centred between two rays, then back to the inner circle.

Weave over these two threads as shown in Fig 216.

Lay all the threads, then work around the circle again, weaving.

Finally work three rounds of loop stitches inside the inner circle, whipping the final round to make an even circle.

Fasten off by threading up through these rounds and a woven triangle.

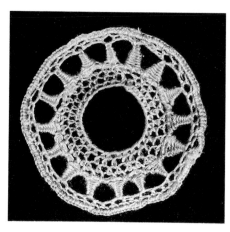

Fig 216 *Woven triangles*

# Woven wheel with picots

With all wheels it is advantageous to have
sufficient thread in the needle when
working a spider or woven wheel to
complete this without having to make
joins.

1. Lay eight rays.
2. Whip back along one to the centre.
   Carefully knot stitch all threads
   together.
3. Weave on these eight threads for about
   a quarter of the length of a ray. At the
   end of each round the needle must be
   taken under two rays to allow the
   weaving to alternate. It will be very
   difficult to make the threads lie flat and
   even unless this is done.
4. Whip along one ray towards the outer
   edge of the circle until the half-way
   point. Knot firmly, then work around
   each ray making a knot stitch, keep the
   thread as taught as possible without
   allowing it to go out of shape. Whip
   twice on this thread between each ray.
5. Work four buttonhole stitches, take
   the thread back and pick up the loop
   between one and two, work six
   buttonhole stitches on this loop to
   form a picot. Work seven more picots
   in this manner.
6. Whip up the ray to the outside of the
   circle, then along to the centre
   between two rays. Take the thread up
   and through the loop between two
   picots and back to the outer edge.
   Continue in a zig-zag formation
   around the circle.
7. Work an equal number of buttonhole
   stitches on each of these laid threads,
   thus forming eight points around the
   circle.

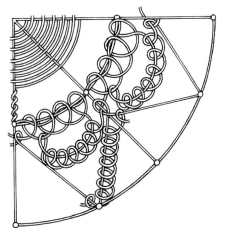

**Fig 217** *Woven wheel with picots*

**Fig 218** *Woven wheel with picots*

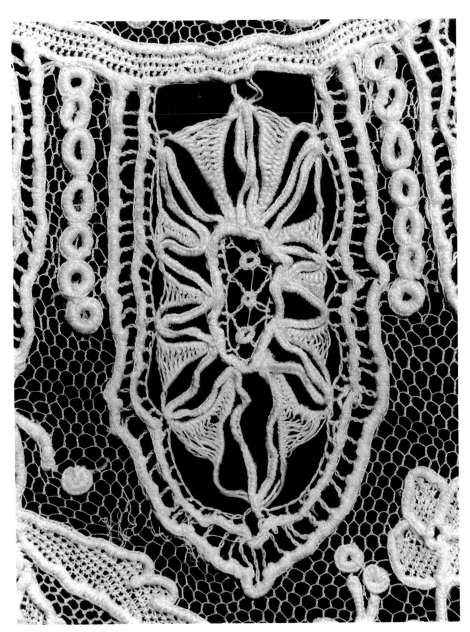

**Fig 219** *An enlarged and elongated woven wheel
filling featured on a piece of Brussels mixed lace
(a dress front, property of Pat Gibson)*

# CHAPTER SEVEN

# Insertions

**Fig 220** *An insertion for a collar, design adapted from a Vogue pattern, featuring many of the stitches in this book. Some interesting insertion stitch ideas (Yvonne Watts, 1986–7)*

## Bar cluster insertion

Fasten the working thread to one long side of the area. Lay straight across and knot stitch into the cordonnet opposite, making sure it is not loose. Work back by overcasting this thread as many times as are needed to achieve a twisted cord appearance. (This depends upon the width of the space and thickness of the chosen thread.)

Work a second bar in the same manner a short distance along the cordonnet.

Work a third bar, but overcast for less than half-way.

Make five buttonhole stitches over the middle of all three bars, then overcast the remainder. The first bar of the next cluster must begin very close to the last, as shown in Fig 222.

## Alençon beads (or bead stitch insertion)

Work evenly spaced stitches along both long edges. It is essential that the stitches are all the same size, opposite one another, and equal in number along both edges.

Fasten the thread to the first loop, then join to the opposite loop by oversewing four times, ensuring that the stitches remain side by side. Do not allow them to overlap.

After the fourth loop, whip around the lower loop. Proceed to the next loop, whip once, then repeat four loops.

**NB:** If working in colours it is possible to do stitches and loops in different shades or colours; also a different thickness of thread could be tried, depending upon the finish desired.

## Bar rosette

Knot stitch to one long edge. Lay the thread diagonally across to the opposite edge, knot stitch, then whip back as in the bar cluster insertion. Whip along the cordonnet, lay across so that the thread crosses diagonally in the centre.

Knot stitch to the opposite edge, whip back along this thread and whip along the cordonnet.

Lay another diagonal, giving six threads crossing in the centre of the space. Whip back to the centre only.

Weave around these threads three or four times, then whip down the remaining diagonal and fasten into the cordonnet.

Repeat, beginning the next diagonal at the finish of the previous one.

**NB:** When weaving with an even number of threads, it is necessary to go under two at the end of each round.

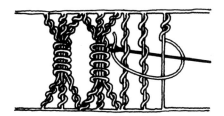

**Fig 221** *Bar cluster*

**Fig 222** *Bar cluster*

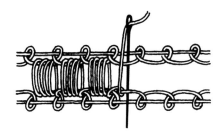

**Fig 223** *Alençon beads*

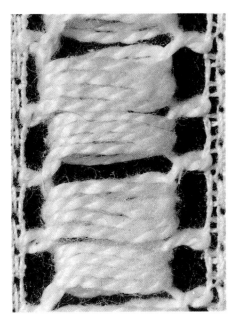

**Fig 224** *Alençon beads*

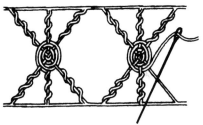

**Fig 225** *Bar rosette*

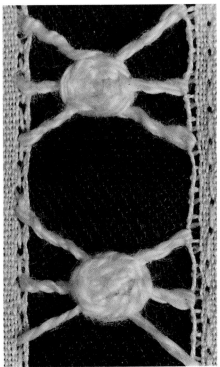

**Fig 226** *Bar rosette*

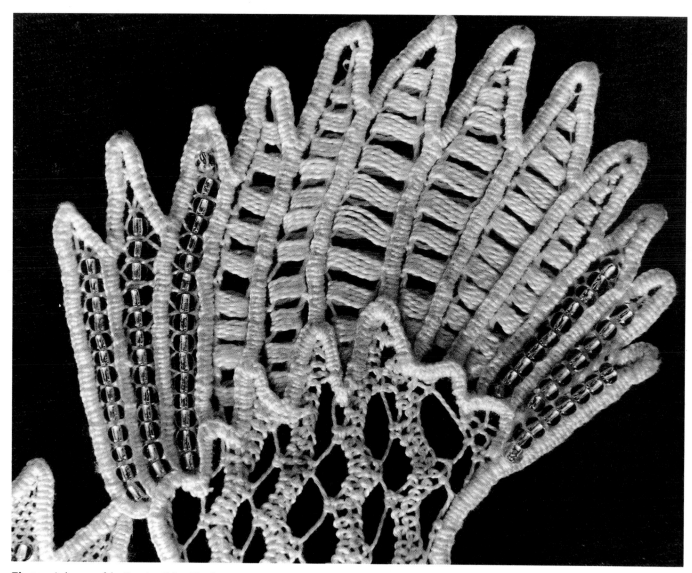

**Fig 227** *A close-up of the Dove's tail (see Fig 1),
showing Alençon beads.*

*Net couronnes (Ros Hills)*

*Decorative rings – stitches on a two-inch diameter*

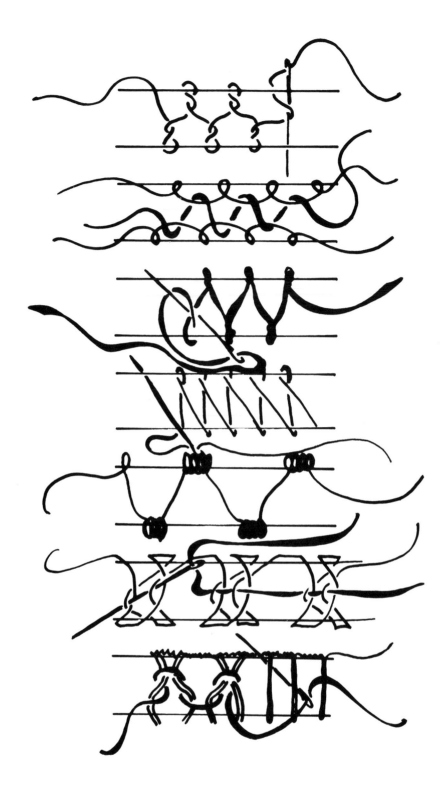

**Fig 228** *Embroidery insertion stitches which could be used in needlelace: a) faggoting, b) laced insertion, c) knotted insertion, d) half cretan stitch, e) buttonhole insertion, f & g) drawn threadwork as insertion stitches*

**Fig 229** *Random insertion stitches into dyed* vilene

*A point de gaze flower worked for the lid of a box,
using space dyed Perle no. 8 and Designer silk, also
incorporating beads of varying size (Pat Gibson,
1987)*

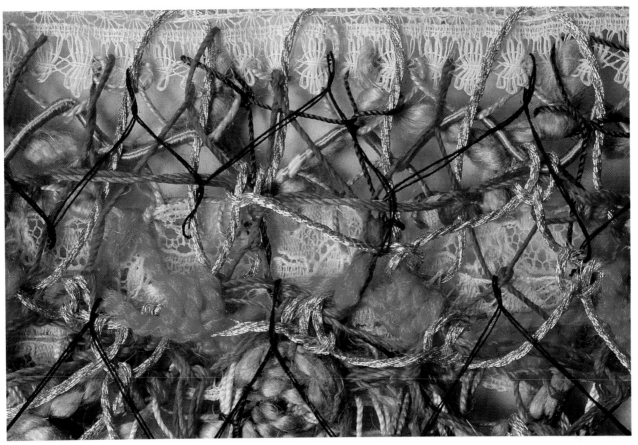

*Random layered stitches (Ros Hills)*

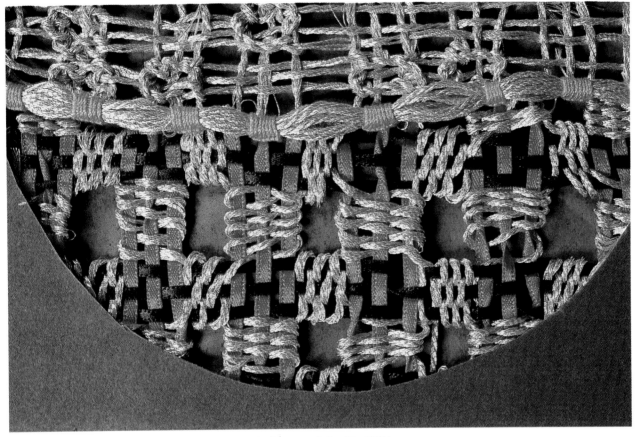

*Grid for purse design (Ros Hills)*

## Brussels stitch squares

Work equally-spaced loop stitches opposite one another along both edges of the area to be filled, as in Alençon beads.

From the mid-way point, work one herringbone stitch into the second loop, then across to the fourth loop on the opposite side.

Continue in this manner on every fourth loop, backwards and forwards until the end is reached.

Repeat to form the squares by returning, thus using every other loop along both edges.

Fasten off the thread.

Rejoin at the top left-hand edge of the first square and work single Brussels stitch across (see Fig 230), whip down the right-hand side and work back into each loop.

Continue to fill the space, but finish with a row worked from left to right in order to begin the next square.

## Plaited insertion stitch

The preparation for this stitch is worked in the same way as for Alençon beads.

The loops are linked across the space by working two, three or four herringbone stitches.

Whip to the next loop and continue.

Try working this stitch in different colours, or, for a more raised effect, use a different textured thread for the herringbone stitches.

## Darned pyramid insertion

(Fig 231)
The alternating pyramids are worked by laying in evenly-spaced herringbone stitches across the space.

Weaving is then worked from the point to the centre of a pyramid.

Transfer the needle across to the next pyramid and continue.

## Inverted darned pyramids

(Fig 231)
Herringbone stitches are worked along the space, placed far apart.

Work a second row in between these.

Weave on the pyramids to the point where they meet in the centre.

## Point d'Angleterre wheel (as featured as one leaf vein)

These are formed as described in chapter 5 but as a single line between two narrow sections of the design. It will be necessary to lay the vertical lines backwards and forwards across the space, then the final line knotting at each point of crossing. Finally weave around these crossed threads two or three times, find the centre and buttonhole over these threads.

## Beads

1. Choose beads that are appropriate for the design.
2. Work a row of single Brussels stitch – each stitch to be the width of a bead – along the space.
3. Thread beads on to the thread before laying it back as in corded stitch. Thread sufficient beads to fill the space on this cord then remove one or two depending upon their size (this is to allow for stitching between them).
4. Whip the thread with beads around the cordonnet, then work a single Brussels stitch around each bead into the first row, fastening into the bottom cordonnet before continuing to the next bead.

In this way all the beads lie evenly along the space.

**NB:** If it is necessary to buttonhole the cordonnet along each edge of the row of beads, take care not to catch the stitching thread around the beads.

**Fig 230** *Insertion of Brussels stitch squares*

**Fig 231** *Insertion of darned pyramid and inverted pyramid*

*One of a pair of tie-ends for a blouse first featured in* Creative Design in Needlepoint Lace *by Nenia Lovesey; featuring Brugge filling and Alençon Beads (Pat Gibson, 1981) 9 cm × 6 cm*

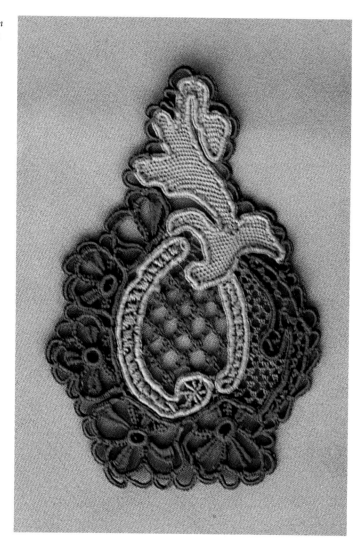

*Another Point de Gaze flower (11 cm × 10 cm) using a thicker cotton embroidery thread and beads (Pat Gibson, 1986)*

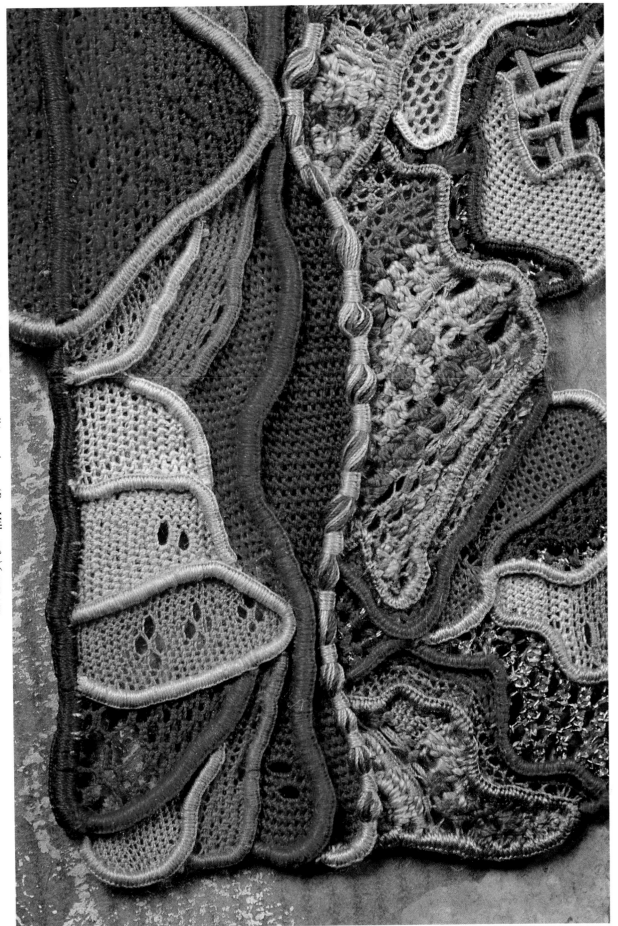

*Ibizan landscape: small 'penny' purse (Ros Hills, 1987) 6 cm × 4 cm.*

**Fig 232** *Line drawing to work in whole or in part.
Sections could be taken out by placing a 'window'
cut out of a sheet of white paper, of perhaps
7 cm × 10 cm, over the design and tracing off the
visible lines*

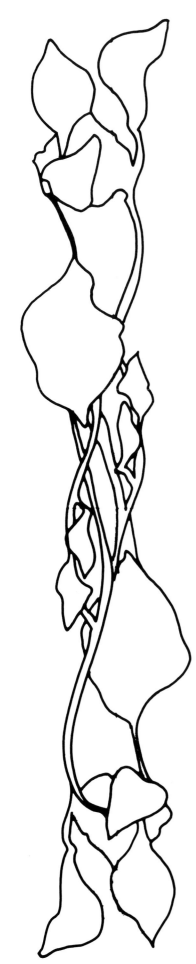

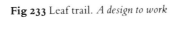
**Fig 233** Leaf trail. *A design to work*

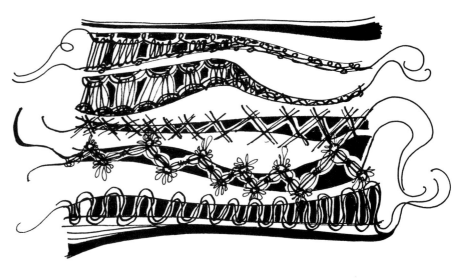

**Fig 234** *Random insertion stitches*

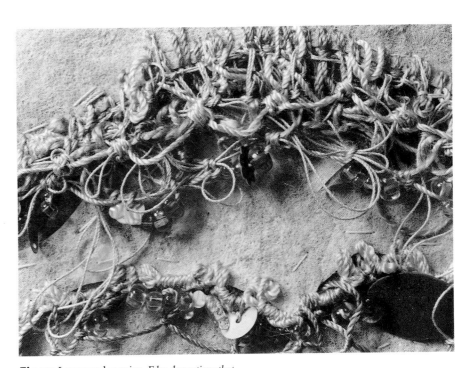

**Fig 235** Loops and sequins. *Edge decorations that could be used around cordonnettes*

*A collection of motifs showing the use of beads and
decorative picots (Pat Gibson, 1985)*

*Belt worked in randomed dyed Designer silk on to a
Dupion silk background, incorporating beads when
working the cordonnette (Pat Gibson, 1988)*

Apache 1. *3D piece using decorative cordonnette
ideas, felt, cotton, silk and paper (Ros Hills, 1988)*

Apache 2. *Cordonnette decorations, paper, silk
and vilene (Ros Hills, 1988)*

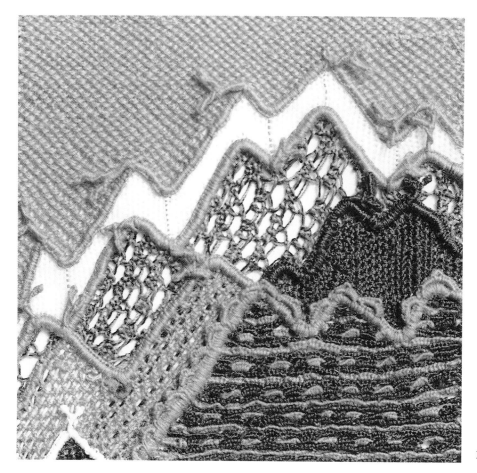

**Fig 236** Hate. *(Jane Meade)* *7 cm × 7 cm*

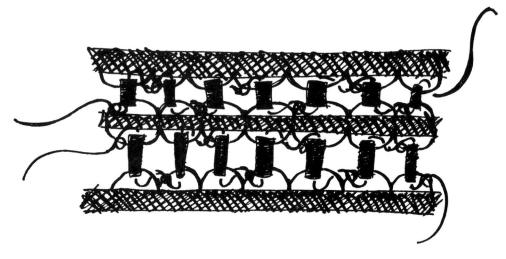

**Fig 237** *Insertion stitch with beads*

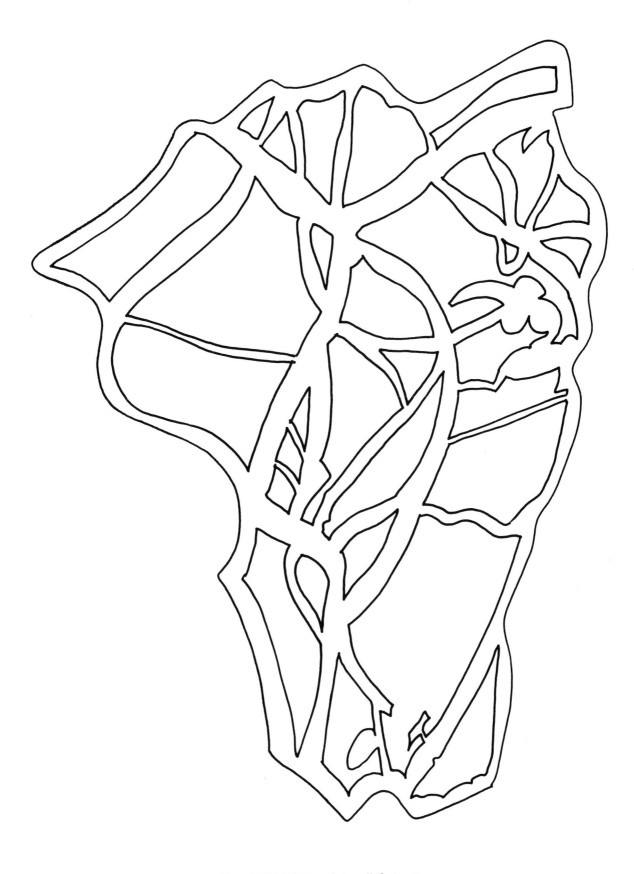

**Fig 238** *This* Life *form design calls for insertion stitchery with the narrow channels between the larger shapes. These larger shapes could be made of needlelace together with sections of stiffened fabric, pelmet* vilene *or felt*

*An enlarged motif using the Venetian gros point techniques (Pat Gibson, 1984) 11 cm × 11.5 cm*

*A motif taken from a piece of Venetian gros point lace, enlarged to 5 cm × 4 cm and worked in 100/3 silk, featuring some different picots as found on the old lace (Pat Gibson, 1986)*

# CHAPTER EIGHT

# Cordonnette decorations and couronnes

## Brides

Bars, brides, bride claires, coxcombs, pearls, legs and ties are all terms used in needlelace for connecting threads worked across spaces.

They may be simply buttonholed or adorned by picots, purls, beads or couronnes.

**Fig 239** *A close-up from a piece of early Alençon needlelace, featuring horsechair in the picots on the flower stems worked directly on to the whipped point d'Espagne ground. The flower (2.5 cm × 3 cm) shows a version of four-hole bud and tiny venetian picots in the centre (0.15 mm across)*

**Fig 240** *A point de gaze flower, the design taken from an old piece of lace, featuring pea stitch variation 1, single corded Brussels stitch, bar cluster and couronnes (Pat Gibson, 1988) 8cm × 7cm*

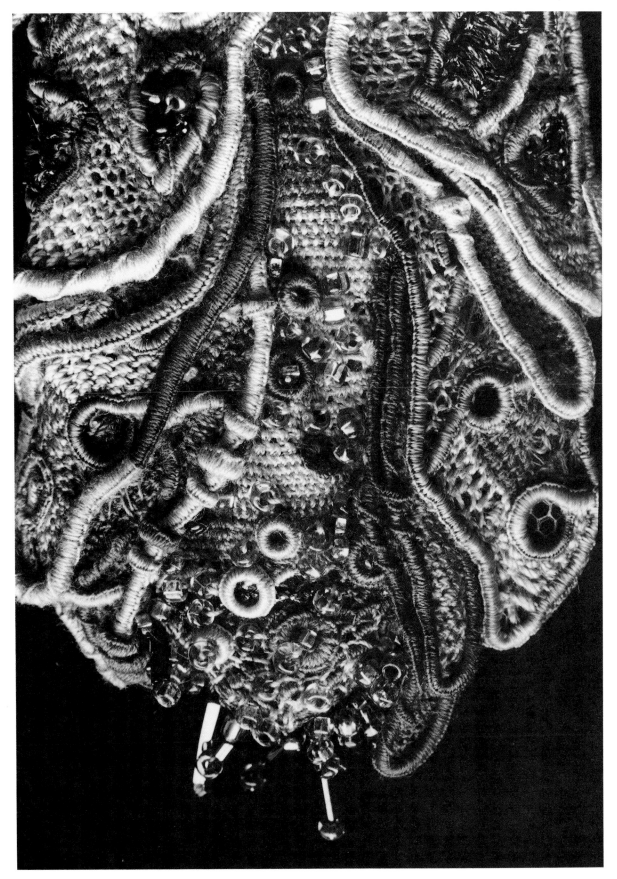

**Fig 241** *Various cordonnette finishes. Purse, Victoria & Albert Museum collection (Ros Hills, 1986)*

## Fil de trace

When working the cordonnette in Venetian gros point, it is necessary to increase the thickness in many areas, thus giving the work a more raised and sculptured appearance. Much of the old Venetian gros point had large numbers of multiples of threads laid in these areas, as many as 50 or 60 in places. Also a thicker, softer thread was often used. This number of threads presents difficulties as regards holding them in position while working the buttonholing. They would also only be very short lengths, as where the design narrows or follows a very tight curve, many of the threads need to be removed. To overcome this problem the la trace is worked as follows (see Fig 242).

Over the area for working, lay in trace threads as shown in the diagram, the longest thread where the cordonnette will be widest, then two or three progressively shorter threads on either side – an odd number in total.

These trace threads are laid in position right through the backing fabric and fastened securely on the back before beginning to thread in the cordonnette threads.

Thread the padding threads through these stitches backwards and forwards as many times as possible, until no more can be included.

This will give a raised and rounded appearance to the finished cordonnette. It will be necessary to lay extra threads over these while buttonholing, to create a smooth finish. The thread lines on the diagram (Fig 242) are only representative of the direction in which the threads are laid under the trace stitches, showing how the shorter threads become filled to capacity first. Many threads would need to be laid in to achieve a very raised and rounded cordonnette.

## The cordonnet or cordonnette

The use of these terms can be most misleading, depending upon which books are used for reference. In this book, the cordonnet refers to the laid thread couched in place around the chosen design, into which the decorative filling stitches are worked. The cordonnette then refers to the raised buttonholed and decorated edgings that are worked over the cordonnet in order to complete the work.

In this chapter we have attempted to cover as many different ways of working the cordonnette as possible.

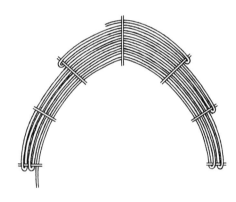

**Fig 242** *Fil de Trace. This diagram shows only the method of laying the threads. It will be appreciated that all the threads cannot be shown*

## Simple cordonnette

This may be worked directly on the couched thread, giving a very fine outline to the work. If two or multiples of two threads are laid around the design, then a totally different appearance will result.

Many other books give adequate instructions for working the cordonnette, therefore here we will pass on to some of the more eleaborate ways of working it, and the decorative devices that are to be found worked both into and over the cordonnette. Some of them are worked as the buttonholing progresses while others, such as couronnes, are worked separately and attached later.

In order to make the cordonnette look as if it is spiralling, make buttonhole stitches in the normal way, but, as you work each loop stitch, ease each one slightly above the other in a diagonal direction until the loops reach the back of the cordonnette (see Fig 245). Pass the needle underneath the cordonnette, bringing it out beside the thread of the last stitch that you made. To continue the spiral, make more loop stitches in the same way. To keep the spirals regular, count the number of loop stitches required each time.

**Fig 243** *Sample of early seventeenth-century Venetian gros point lace showing gros point diamond stitch, heavily padded cordonnette, and tight ring picots*

**Fig 244** *A mat sampler based on a Honiton lace design, showing a selection of different filling stitches (Worked by Pat Gibson for a weekend workshop, 1985)*

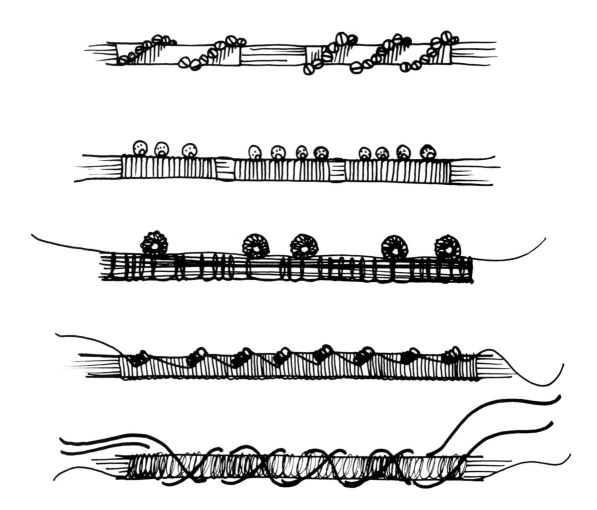

**Fig 245** *Cordonnette decorations: a) spiral
cordonnette with beads, b) cordonnette with the
stitch knot at the top of the cord, with beads,
c) spaced buttonhole stitches with buttonhole rings
upright on the top of the cord (these rings may be
made after the initial buttonholing using a support,
i.e. a ringstick or darning needle), d) spaced
buttonhole stitch on cord with groups of four
buttonhole stitches added to the top of the cord,
e) after buttonhole stitches have been made over core
of laid threads whip around the cord with metallic
threads*

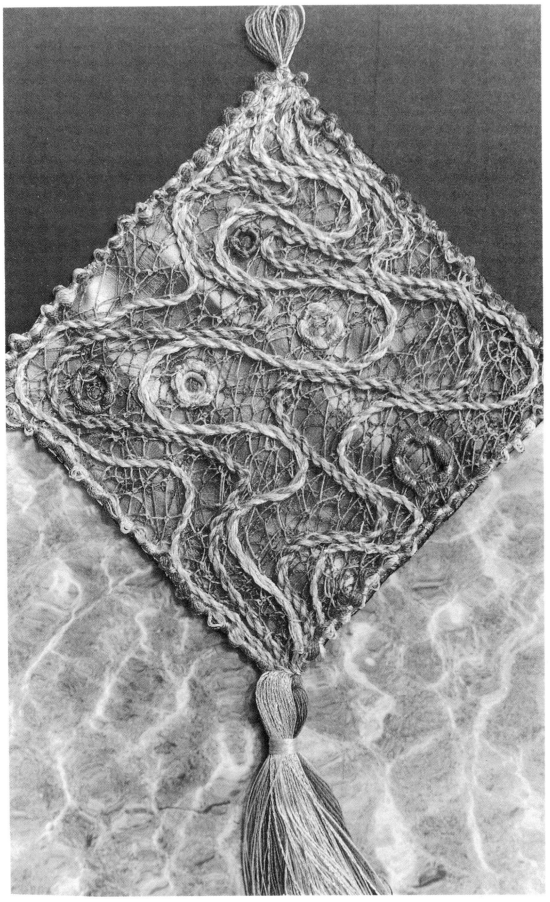

**Fig 246** Love *(Jane Meade, 1988)*

## Ring picot

This picot is usually worked as the buttonholing of the cordonnette progresses. It is possible to add picots after completing the cordonnette, but the number of strands will have to be adjusted as will be explained later.

Work past the beginning of a picot, preferably by a set number of stitches which should then remain constant, in order to keep the picots the same size.

Take the working thread back by this number. Pass the needle through the appropriate loop from beneath, back to the loop of the last stitch and back again (three loops laid).

Buttonhole on these threads as many times as will fill the loops comfortably.

Continue buttonholing along the cordonnette for the set number of stitches and repeat with the next picot.
**NB:** When buttonholing, the loops will appear to stretch slightly – tension will only be achieved with practice, but it is advisable to pull the loops tighter than would at first appear necessary.

It is possible to work numerous variations with this ring picot (Fig 248) as shown by Fig 256.

If picots are to be added when the cordonnette is complete, then an even number of strands will have to be laid, otherwise the work cannot proceed in the same direction.

All of these picots may be decorated by incoporating beads at the centre point, or working more picots upon them.

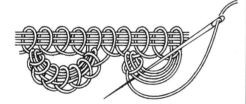

**Fig 248** *Ring picot*

## Single loop picot

Work from left to right.

Buttonhole along the cordonnette to the required point for the picot.

Place a pin into the backing fabric, or straight into the pillow.

Take the working thread down and around the pin then up and over the cordonnet.

Pass the needle from left to right behind the two threads around the pin.

Pass the working thread under and over the point of the needle to form a knot.

Pull up tightly on the cordonnet.

Continue buttonholing along to the point for the next picot.

The pin may be removed after working a few more stitches.
Simply reverse the direction if the picot is being worked from right to left (Fig 249a).

## Venetian picot

These are found in profusion on much of the early Venetian needlelace, in particular Venetian gros point, rose point and point de neige.

The picots are longer than the single loop picot, and appear to be more rigid. It is possible to make them to any length, by placing the pin as for a single picot at any preferred spot. It will be noted that after every fourth or fifth stitch, the picot will twist. The longer the picot, the great the number of twists. They are useful devices for the antennae of butterflies and other such insects!

1. Work the cordonnette to the required position.
2. Place a pin in the work or pillow as far from the cordonnette as required.
3. Take the working thread down around the pin, over the cordonnet and around the pin again from left to right.

**Fig 247** *A brooch worked with an extra petal, featuring beads instead of spaces in single corded Brussels stitch, Point de Valencienne on the extra petal and ring picots around the edge. (Pat Gibson, 1982) 5.5cm diameter*

4. Make the first buttonhole over the first two strands as shown in Fig 250a or b, then buttonhole over all three back towards the cordonnet. (If the first stitch is worked over all three laid threads, it has a tendency to slide over the end when the pin is removed. The picot then comes undone!)

5. Continue working the cordonnette until arriving at the position for the next picot, then repeat.

Fig 250c shows the completed picot. Fig 250a shows how to work the picot from right to left.

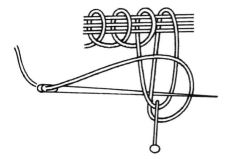

**Fig 250a** *Venetian picot, right to left*

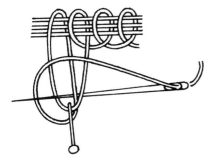

**Fig 250b** *Venetian picot, left to right*

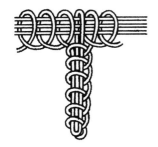

**Fig 250c** *Venetian picot, the completed stitch*

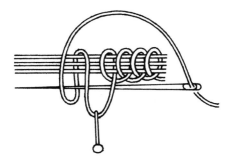

**Fig 249a** *Single picot, right to left*

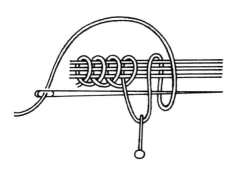

**Fig 249b** *Single picot, left to right*

**Fig 251** *Enlargement from a piece of early Alençon needlelace, featuring insertions with tiny Venetian picots, and a central mesh with longer Venetian picots and buttonholed bars. (Each picot 0.1 cm and whole motif 2.4 cm × 2.5 cm)*

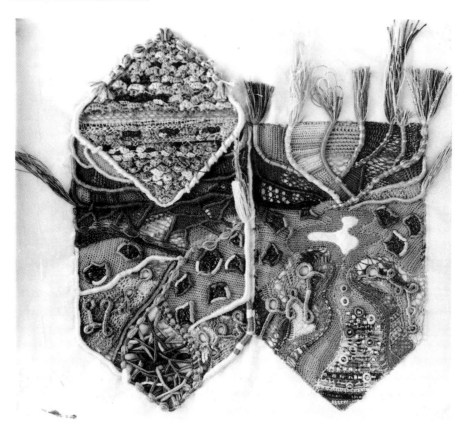

Fig 252 *Purse in progress. The photograph shows the work still attached to the architects' linen base with the cordonnette being attached (Ros Hills, 1987)*

Fig 254 Venetia. *Make a double loop stitch ground. Bring a contrast thread and whip around loops of double loop stitch to chosen position of picot. Make subsequent picots at random on the face of the work*

**Fig 253** Venetia. *Enlarged diagram to show Venetian picots on a double loop stitch ground*

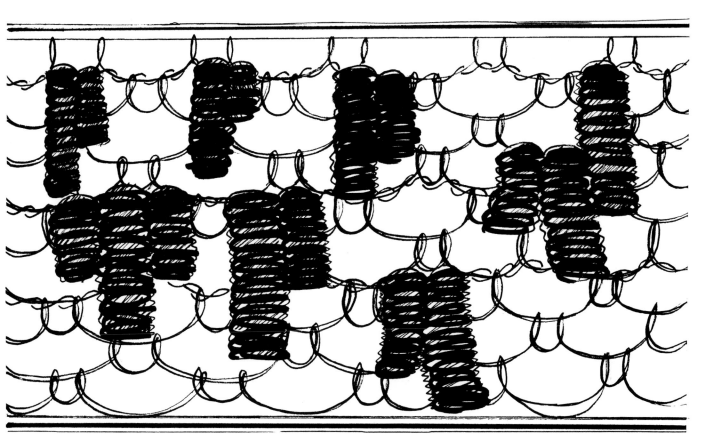

## Chain stitch picot

This gives a much less formal picot, with a looser appearance.

Buttonhole, as with all picots, to the required position.

Put the needle into the loop with the working thread passing behind the point of the needle (Fig 255).

Pull up the loop, but place the needle into the new loop before tightening. Continue working chain stitches in this manner until the desired length is achieved.

Take the needle behind and back into the cordonnet. Continue buttonholing.

## Bullion picot

At the desired point, take the needle back through the loop of the last stitch, and wrap the thread at least six times (more if necessary) around the needle evenly. Do not pull them too tightly. Hold the threads with a finger while easing the needle through, then work the next buttonhole stitch into the cordonnet.

(This will require practice, particularly to establish the number of twists required to give a rounded loop.)

**Fig 255** *Chain stitch picot*

**Fig 256** *Chain stitch picot and series of ring picots with a single loop picot at the apex of the triangle*

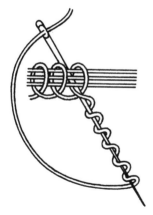

**Fig 257a** *Bullion knot working*

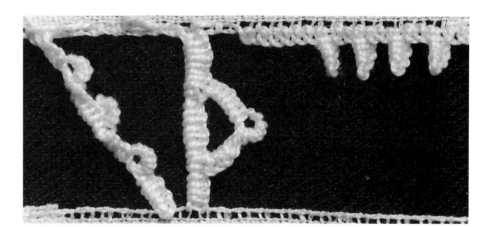

**Fig 258** *Bullion knot picots, venetian picots and buttonhole bars often used to join sections of lace together, with or without picots of the worker's choice*

**Fig 257b** *Bullion knot, the completed stitch*

**Fig 260** *Point plat. Showing an elaborately raised cordonnette worked after the original lace was completed, featuring ring picots and Venetian picots*

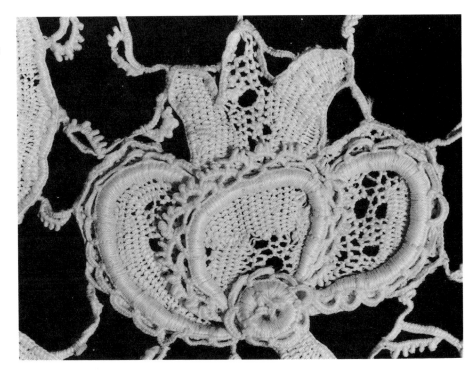

**Fig 259** *A single motif from a piece of Venetian Gros Point lace, early seventeenth century, featuring bullion knots, ring picots and a heavily padded cordonnette*

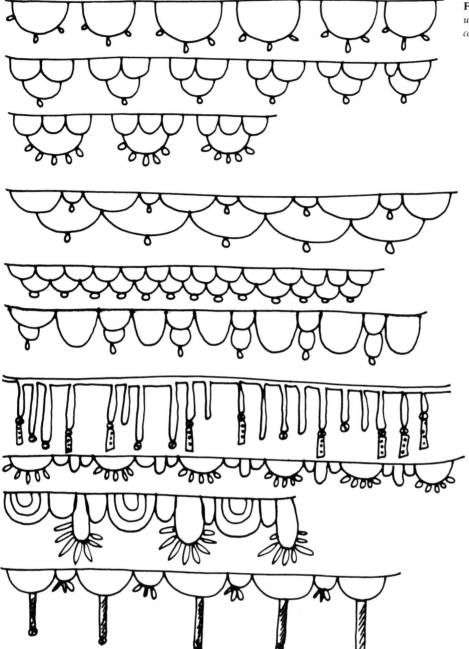

**Fig 261** *Edges. Picots of different types are used with beads to form decorative edges on the cordonnette*

**Fig 262** *Random stitched edges. Decorate the cordonnette with a wide variety of flaps, beads, sequins, long loops and groups of stitches*

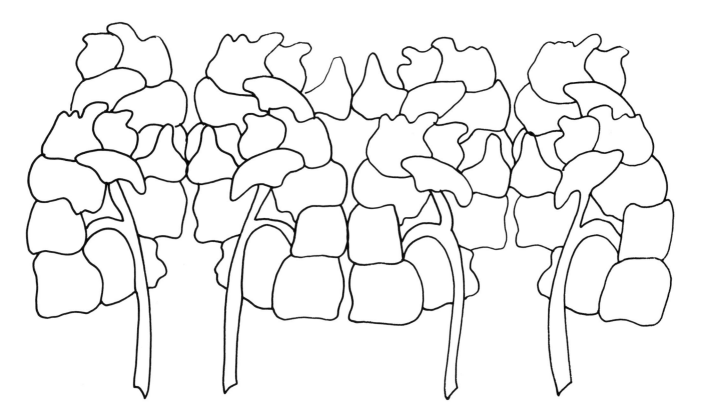

**Fig 263** Flower shapes. *A design to work*

## Couronnes

'An ornament to the cordonnette, and used in Needle Point laces. The couronnes are either worked as a decoration to the cordonnette that forms the edge of the lace, or round any raised cordonnettes in the body of the pattern; when in the later position, they with Spines and Thorns, are known as Fleurs Volantes' (S.F.A. Caulfield, *Encyclopaedia of Victorian Needlework*).

The couronnes, or rings, are worked separately and sewn into position using stab stitches. They may be attached after the completed work is removed from the backing fabric or while it is still in place. They are placed in the centre of flowers or at the base of a design where several fillings meet. They may be of different shapes and sizes, plain or ornamented with picots, and in some cases several of varying sizes may be placed on top of each other.

It is advisable to experiment first with several different types to establish the overall effect that is required. Any couronnes made and found to be either the wrong size or superfluous, should be kept for possible use on another project. Stitch them on to a single thread so as not to lose them, or treat yourself to one of the attractive wooden couronne boxes available today.

## Working a couronne

Using a ringstick: A selection of different sized knitting needles may be used for this purpose. On the other hand, there are many attractive needlework tools being made today, many of them reproductions of the old style tools, and it is very satisfying to both own and use these.

1. Ascertain the size of ring required by laying the ringstick over the centre of the design area to be covered. The sides of the ringstick should fit within the circumference of the circle. The thickness of the padding and buttonholing will take up the rest of the space.

   Thread a needle with a long length of thread. Wrap the end several times – at least four, and many more for a thicker ring – around the desired size.

   Make a single buttonhole stitch while it is still on the ringstick (this to hold all the threads together).

   Gently push the threads down the stick or needle, grip with the thumb and first finger and remove completely.

   Alternatively, push the ring on to the next smaller ring on the stick, and buttonhole around it while still held in place.

   Buttonhole completely around the ring, pushing the stitches close together to make sure they are well packed.

2. It is sometimes difficult to get the needle through the threads, while wrapped around the ringstick, in order to begin the buttonholing.

   Lay the needle on the ringstick (having first selected the next smallest size to that originally chosen) with its point towards the end, wrap the end of thread *not* in the eye of the needle around the ringstick the required number of times, then once around the point of the needle, and pull out the needle. This makes the first stitch while still on the ringstick.

All couronnes may be decorated by any of the methods described or illustrated as in Fig 264.

## Tiny couronnes

Very tiny couronnes can present problems mainly in holding while buttonholing around them.

It is possible to use very fine knitting needles or one of the tiny ring sticks now being made, but the problem of holding the threads still arises. However, one way of overcoming this problem is to work them attached to the architect's linen, pinned to the pillow.

Place a dot on the pillow then, using a sharp sewing needle, work four La Trace stitches at right angles to each other around the dot. Ensure that the stitches are all the same length.

Fasten off this thread on the back.

Rejoin with the colour required for the couronne and thread through the Trace threads until they are full. It is then only necessary to buttonhole around these threads as for a normal couronne.

The usual decorative devices; e.g. picots, beads, etc, can be added as the work proceeds.

These couronnes may be left attached until they are required, as there is then less chance of losing them. Simply snip the trace threads at the back to remove them, and attach in the usual manner.

## Overlapping picots

Work the beginning of the couronne as described above.

Buttonhole around the circle, working eight stitches. Lay the threads back to the first loop, leaving very little slack, back to the eighth loop, back to the first – hence three strands.

Buttonhole on these three as many times as will fill the loop, then continue around the main thread for four stitches.

Lay the three threads back so that they pick up a loop in the middle of the last picot over the top. Buttonhole over these, continue for four more stitches, pick up the last stitch of the first picot and continue.

The picots will form so that they overlap on top of each other.

The last one must be worked by going behind the first in order to keep the sequence correct.

Two colours or more may be used by running the ones not required underneath the buttonholing and bringing them out as needed.

Beads may also be sewn to the middle of the picot as the work progresses.

## Half-couronne

These couronnes may be worked over the cordonnette, or directly on a piece of flat stitching, e.g. single corded Brussels stitch for the leaf vein (Fig 141).

Lay a ringstick or fine knitting needle over the position where the couronne is required.

Bring the working thread up from behind the work, over the ringstick and back behind the work again.

Repeat these windings as many times as are required to give the necessary thickness.

Buttonhole closely over all these threads, either on the ringstick or not, as preferred, until the level of base stitches is reached. Take the working thread through to the back of the work.

If placing these couronnes on to the cordonnette, run the needle carefully through the existing buttonholing, until arriving at the point for the next couronne.

These couronnes may also be embellished with beads and other picots.

**Fig 264** *A sampler showing many couronnes (Pat Gibson)*

**Fig 265** *A enlargement of the Dove's eye from Fig 1, showing overlapping picots with beads worked on to the couronne*

## Rosie stitch

1. Make a dense ground of corded stitch.
2. Bring a thicker thread from the side of the space you are working in underneath the ground and up through the stitches to the front of the work at the chosen point.
3. Using a support (i.e. a ring stick, darning needle or pencil, depending on the scale of the work) laid on the work at the point where the thicker thread comes through the corded stitch, wrap the thicker thread around the support. Take it down through the corded stitch and then up again and around the support. Do this several times to create a ring.
4. Buttonhole stitch the ring thus created.
5. Remove the support and pass the thick thread down through the corded stitch ground. Bring it up again where you want another ring to start.

**Fig 267** *Rosie stitch*

**Fig 266** *Rosie stitch*

**Fig 268** Bubbles. *A design to work*

**Fig 269** *Couronnes – detail from a needlelace hanging by Carla Aarts, Holland, combining lace and pieces of fabric*

**Fig 270** *This tiny motif (1.5 cm × 1.5 cm) features gros point diamond stitch in its original form, also Venetian picots around ring picots (see enlarged couronne in Fig 264)*

**Fig 271** *An enlargement of a wheel with numerous couronnes, from a piece of point de gaze (3 cm × 3 cm)*

**Fig 272** *Another petal, featuring four-hole bud, beads on the ring picots, Venetian picots on the centre couronne and spider wheel filling (Pat Gibson, 1982)*

**Fig 273** *A flower design worked on a belt, showing many of the basic stitches, spiralling on the cordonnette, Venetian picots with a variety of beads (Pat Gibson, 1988). 18 cm × 9 cm*

**Fig 274** *Purse. Small purse made in silk thread
with ribbon hanging cord decorated with beads.
A silk tassel completes this charming picture
(Pam Nether)*

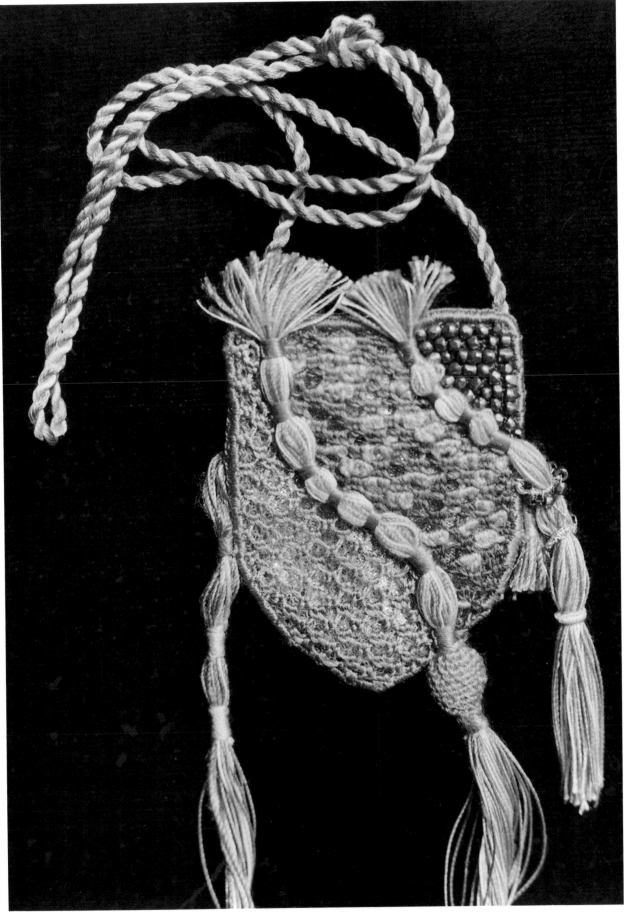

**Fig 275** *Purse. This photograph shows a
cordonnette with spaced buttonhole stitches
revealing a multicoloured core thread
(Ann Dolphin, 1986)*

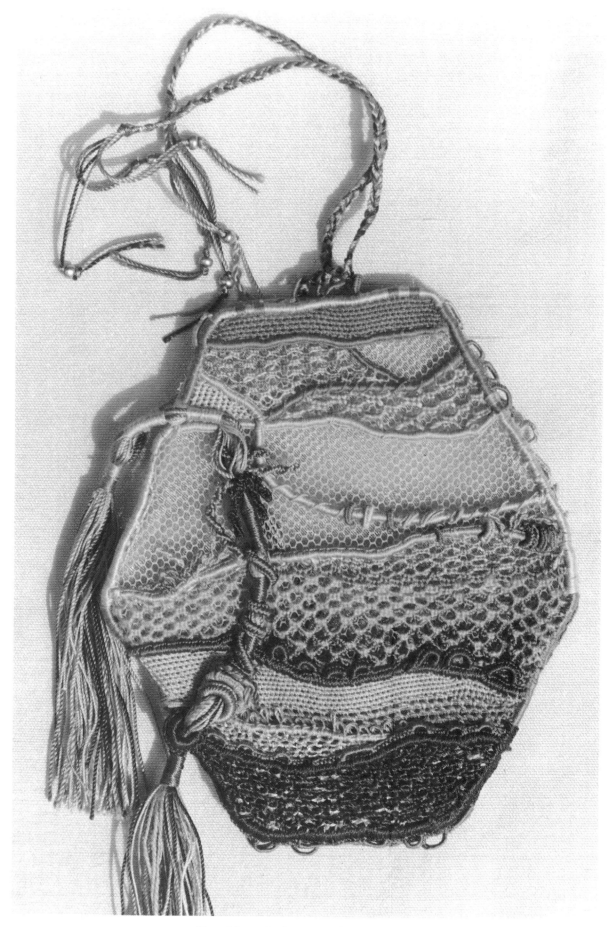

**Fig 276** *Purse. Cordonnettes are decorated with*
*rings and spiral cordonnette (Maureen O' Dwyer)*

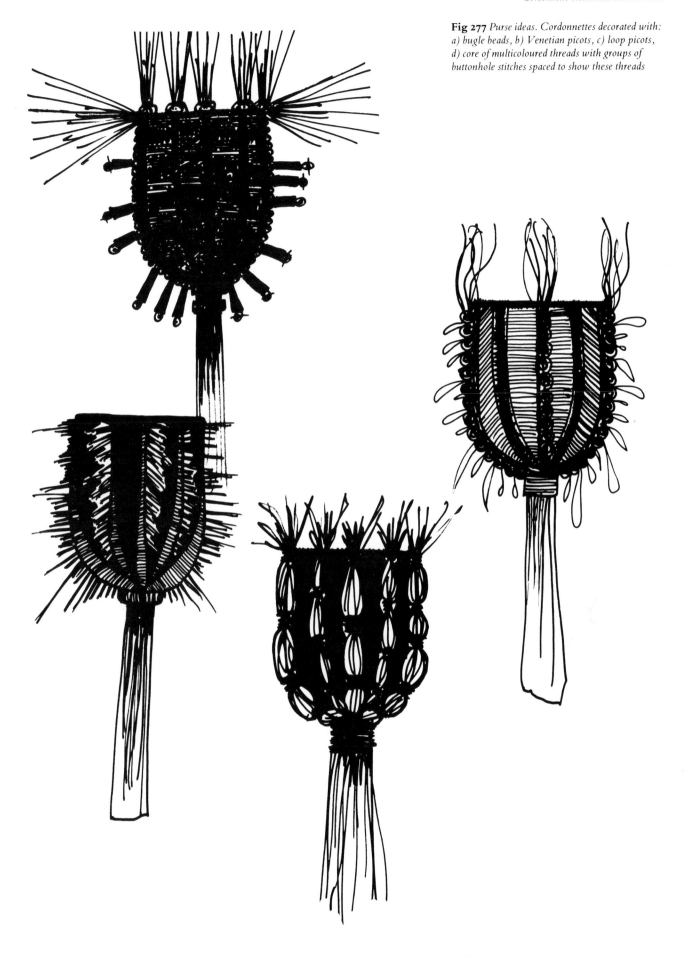

**Fig 277** *Purse ideas. Cordonnettes decorated with:
a) bugle beads, b) Venetian picots, c) loop picots,
d) core of multicoloured threads with groups of
buttonhole stitches spaced to show these threads*

**Fig 278** *Purse ideas. a) stripes of different colours,*
*b) buttonhole stitches varying in degree of spacing,*
*c) small strips of fabric or pieces of thread included*
*in the buttonhole stitches, d) a spiralled cordonnette*
*with beads.*

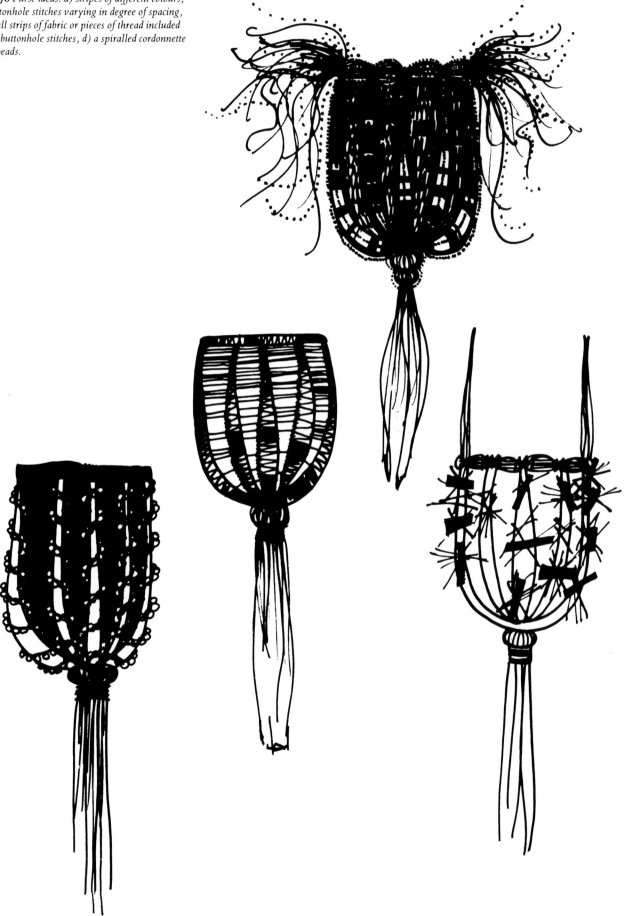

# Suppliers

Alby Lace Centre
Cromer Road
Alby
Norwich
Norfolk

Frank Herring & Sons
27 High West Street
Dorchester
DT1 1UP

Loricraft
4 Big Lane
Lambourn
Berks RG16 7XQ

Honiton Lace Shop
44 High Street
Honiton
Devon

Mace and Nairn
89 Crane Street
Salisbury
Wilts

The Lace Guild
The Hollies
53 Audnam
Stourbridge
West Midlands
DY8 4AE

D. H. Shaw
47 Zamor Crescent
Thurscroft
Rotherham
South Yorks

John & Jennifer Ford
October Hill
Upper Way
Upper Longdon
Rugeley
Staffs WS15 1QB

Shireburn Lace
Finkle Court
Finkle
Serburn in Elmet
North Yorks

Enid Taylor
Valley House Craft Studio
Ruston
Scarborough
North Yorks
YO13 9QE

George White
Delaheys Cottage
Thistle Hill
Knaresborough
North Yorks

English Lace School
Oak House
Church Stile
Woodbury
near Exeter
Devon

D. J. Hornsby
149 High Street
Burton Latimer
Kettering
Northants
NN15 5RL

Liz Bartlett
12 Creslow Court
Galley Hill
Stony Stratford
MK11 1NN

Sebalace
Waterloo Mill
Howden Road
Silsden
West Yorks BD20 0HA

T. Brown
Woodside
Greenlands Lane
Prestwood
Great Missenden
Bucks

A. Sells
49 Pedley Lane
Clifton
Shefford
Beds

C. & D. Springett
21 Hillmorton Road
Rugby
Warks CV22 5DF

B. Phillips
Pantglas
Cellen
Lampeter
Dyfed

Newnham Lace Equipment
11 Dorchester Close
Basingstoke
Hants RG23 8EX

A. L'Econome
Anne-Marie Deydier
Ecole de Dentelle aux Fuseaux
10 rue Paul Chenavard
69001 Lyon
France

Heikina de Ruyter
Feldohlentrup 22
4933 Blomber/Lippe
West Germany

Bartlett, Caesar & Partners
The Glen
Downton
Lymington
Hants

# Bibliography

*Point Lace*, Mlle Riego de la Blanchardière, 1869
*Studies in Modern Lacemaking*, Butterick Publishing Company, 1898
*Old Point Lace and how to copy it*, Daisy Waterhouse Hawkins, 1878
*The New Lace Embroidery*, L. A. Tebbs, Chapman & Hall, 1905
*Supplement to the New Punto Tagliato Embroidery*, L. & R. Tebbs, 1913
*Encyclopedia of Needlework*, Therese de Dillmont, Mullhouse

*Lace*, Virginia Churchill Bath, Studio Vista
*Colour and Texture in Needlelace*, Ros Hills, Dryad Press
*Needlelace in Photographs*, Cynthia Voysey, B. T. Batsford
*Needlemade Laces*, Pat Earnshaw, Ward Lock
*Venetian Gros Point Lace*, Nenia Lovesey & Catherine Barley, Dryad Press
*Punto Tagliato Lace*, Nenia Lovesey, Dryad Press

Additional books for design inspiration:
*Colour*, edited by Helen Varley, Marshall Editions
*Architectural Stained Glass*, edited by Brian Clarke, John Murray
*Fibre Arts Design Book 2*, Lark Books
*Textile Crafts*, edited by Constance Howard, Pitman
*Embroidery and Colour*, Constance Howard, Batsford
Dover range of design motif books

# Index